Owen B. Maginnis

Practical centring

Treating of the Practice of centring Arches in building Construction as

carried on in the United States at the present Time

Owen B. Maginnis

Practical centring
Treating of the Practice of centring Arches in building Construction as carried on in the United States at the present Time

ISBN/EAN: 9783337106157

Printed in Europe, USA, Canada, Australia, Japan

Cover: Foto ©ninafisch / pixelio.de

More available books at **www.hansebooks.com**

PRACTICAL CENTRING

TREATING OF THE PRACTICE OF

CENTRING ARCHES

In Building Construction as carried on in the United
States at the Present Time

ALSO

GIVING OTHER USEFUL INFORMATION OF VALUE
TO THE TRADE

BY

OWEN B. MAGINNIS

SIXTY-FIVE ILLUSTRATIONS

NEW YORK
WILLIAM T. COMSTOCK, PUBLISHER
No. 23 WARREN STREET
1891

INTRODUCTION.

IN response to a request from many carpenters and builders to republish in book form the following articles, which originally appeared in *Carpentry and Building*, *The National Builder*, and *The American Builder*, all published in the United States, and in the *Illustrated Carpenter and Builder*, published in London, England, I now take pleasure in putting forth this little volume, with the hope that they will find it useful.

The work embraces each subject in detail, and in language that practical men can understand. I would especially commend it to the attention of students attending trade, technical, and architectural schools, as they will find it helpful in acquiring the practical knowledge of construction so essential to success.

My best thanks are due to the builders, from whom I have obtained much of my information; also to the publisher, who has gotten up the book in a form to be a useful addition to the chest or book-shelf of every rising worker in the trade.

OWEN B. MAGINNIS.

NEW YORK, 1891.

CONTENTS.

CHAPTER VIII.

PRACTICAL CENTRING.

CHAPTER I.

PRACTICAL CENTRING.—CENTRES OF FIREPLACES OR BRICK LINTELS.
—CENTRES FOR SEGMENTAL ARCHES OF SMALL SPAN, SHOWING
METHODS OF CONSTRUCTION.

CENTRING may be described as an auxiliary art employed by masons in building construction for the purpose of sustaining temporarily the voussoirs, or pieces of stone or brick which form an arch, holding them in their correct position until the last, or keying piece, is inserted, and the whole arch has had time to settle into place. The temporary supports used are called "centres," and are usually supplied by the carpenter. It devolves upon him to put them in correct position under the intended arch whenever required by the mason. Centres, accordingly, must be constructed of correct shape, and in a way to have sufficient strength, both by nature of the form and the material employed, to resist the weight which is to be placed upon them. The centres must be firmly fixed in place, and yet, as they are only for temporary use, provision must be made for gradually lowering them for the purpose of taking them out when they have fulfilled their mission. There are many kinds of centres required for the different designs of arches which are constructed, reaching from the simple brick lintel to the complex groin. All of these demand care in their design and construction.

In an attempt to illustrate principles and show methods of construction I will commence at the simplest form—

namely, that which is illustrated in Fig. 1 of the accompanying sketches. While this example may be considered elementary, and is certainly easy to understand, it, in fact,

FIG. 1.—Simple Fireplace.

involves the whole system of centring. The view represents an open cavity or fireplace, 2 ft. 6 in. wide, and 3 ft. high, over which the bricklayer has to build an arch, or, as it is commonly called, "extend a brick lintel." To construct the centre necessary for this purpose the carpenter would use first a piece of ¼ in. pine somewhat longer than the width of the opening between the jambs, and would joint one of its edges. He would then square across both ends $\frac{1}{16}$ in. shorter than the width of the opening, and draw a line parallel to and 1 in. removed from the jointed edge, all as shown in Fig. 2 of the illustrations. He would then divide the length into two equal parts, and square across the division point. Then, laying the piece of board

FIG. 2.—Getting the Curve.

down on the bench, and tacking it there, he would drive three nails, as shown in the sketch, one at each springing point, or where the curve cuts the parallel line already referred to. He would drive one also at the crown or middle point, as indicated. He would then bend a pliable lath around the three nails and mark by it the required curve of

the arch. He would next saw out clean this line, using for
the purpose a compass saw or band saw, in case the work
is being done where such a machine is available. He
would also saw across with the square lines, and would
finally clean the curved edge neatly. By this means the
mould would be secured for the centre, or for several cen-

FIG. 3.—Another form of Centre.

tres, if more than one be needed. In preparing the piece
for the centre, this mould would be used on both sides of
a piece of 2 in. by 4 in. stuff, marking the desired shape.
This would then be sawed to the line and cross-cut on the
square lines, resulting in the same shape as the mould
already described. The resulting piece would be the centre on which the arch would be turned, having a rise, according to the conditions already mentioned, of 1 in. The
length of the uprights to be used under the arch would be
2 ft. 11 in. This added, to the thickness of the centre, 1
in., already mentioned, would give 3 ft. to the springing
line. Another form of centre sometimes employed is illustrated in Fig. 3. This is worked to triangular form, the
curve being added by means of mortar put in place by the
mason as he lays his brick. Arches built this way, however, are not so satisfactory as when laid upon centres finished to the exact curve required.

FIG. 4.—Centre and Supporters.

To set the centre the carpenter would proceed as follows:
He would construct the frame shown in Fig. 4 (the up-

rights are 1 in. by 4 in.), and would place in the opening in
Fig. 1, keeping the front edges of the upright flush with
the face of the brickwork. Two braces would be driven
in, as shown in Fig. 4, between the uprights, to hold them
fast against the jambs. The centre would then be cor-

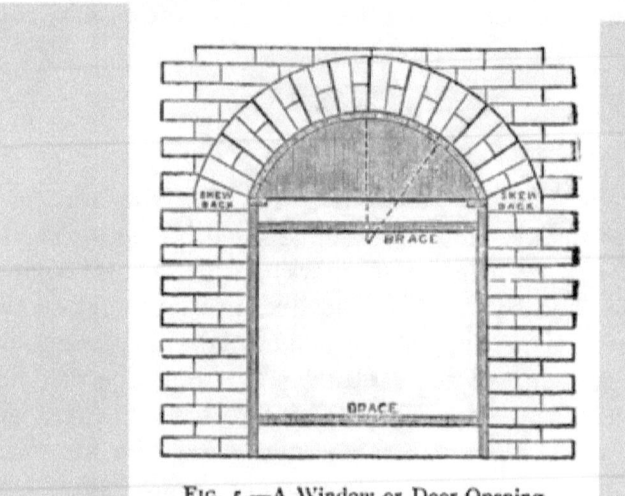

FIG. 5.—A Window or Door Opening.

rectly levelled by applying the spirit level to the bottom
side of the centre. Whichever side was too low would be
furred up. The mason would then proceed to turn the
arch, as shown in Fig. 1. To ease the centre the braces
would first be gently knocked out, and then the bottom
ends of the uprights would be forced outward from the

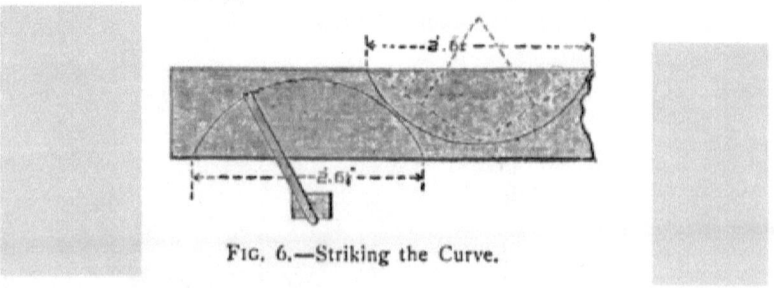

FIG. 6.—Striking the Curve.

jambs towards the middle of the opening. By this means
the arch would be lowered uniformly.

Fig. 5 represents a segmental arch spanning a door or
window. It may be assumed to be 2 ft. 8 in. wide, with a

rise of 12 in., and the wall may be assumed to be 8 in. thick. To make a centre of this kind the carpenter would proceed as follows: A sound rough board 1 in. thick, equal in width to the rise—that is, 12 in.—would be used in the manner shown in Fig. 6. The centre by which to construct the curve would be found as shown to the right. The curve would be struck by means of a trammel, or, in the absence of this, a rod would be cut equal to the radius of the curve. A brad awl would be driven through the centre of the rod, a block being placed under for the purpose of raising it up to the thickness of the board, and the curve described as shown at the left in Fig. 6. The springing line in this case would be 2 ft. 6¼ in. long, or 1¾ in. less

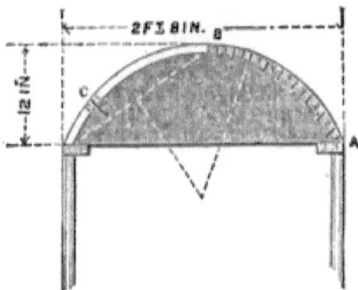

FIG. 7.—Construction of the Centre.

than the length of the arch, in order to allow for the thickness of the battens forming the top of the arch. These would be ⅞ in. in thickness, and one of them would come on each side, thus making it necessary to allow twice seven-eighths. After the curve had been struck in this manner the carpenter would cut the piece out of the board, clean the curved edge neatly to the line, and, using this as a pattern, mark out as many as might be required for the number of arches to be constructed. A pair would be necessary for each centre. Standing the curved pieces on their bottom edges, as shown in Fig. 7, parallel to each other, and 8 in. apart, measuring between outside faces, the workman would next tack on three battens, as shown at A, B, and C in Fig. 7. He would use for this purpose 8d.

common nails.   Then, commencing at point A, he would
nail on the other battens, putting them ½ in. apart,
and keeping their ends flush with the face of the curved
pieces, all as indicated in Fig. 8.   For the purpose of ac-

FIG. 8.—Bottom View of Centre.

curately spacing the batten, a piece of ½ in. stuff about 10
in. long would be used.   Two cleats would also be nailed
across the bottom edges of the curved pieces, as indicated
in Figs. 5 and 8, their purpose being to form a rest for the

FIG. 9.—Top View of Centre.

centre on the top of the uprights.   Figs. 8 and 9 show the
top and bottom view of the centre, constructed as described, and indicates the position of the uprights which
are used to support it.

CHAPTER II.

CONTINUING the consideration of centres for supporting segmental arches from 3 ft. span and upward, an arch is shown at Fig. 10 turned on its neces-

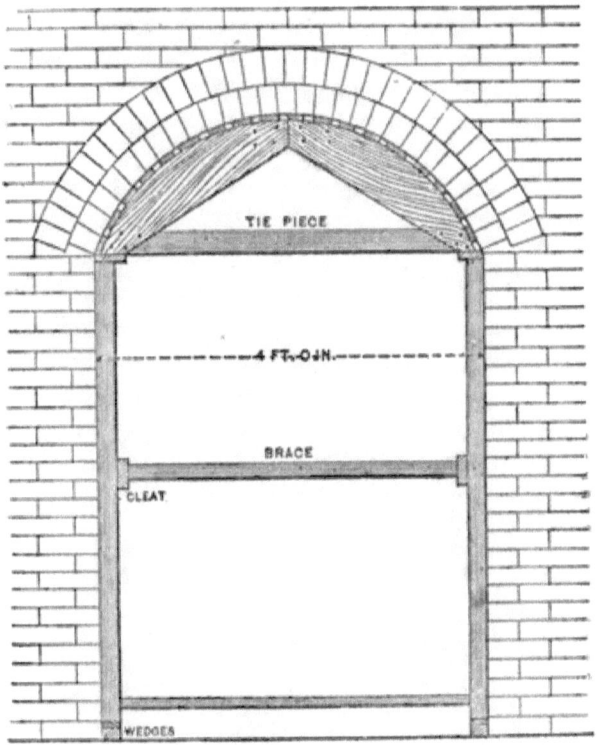

TIE PIECE

4 FT. 0 IN.

BRACE

CLEAT

WEDGES

FIG. 10.—Simple Segmental Arch with Centre in place.

sary centre. The construction of this centre is a matter of more difficulty and labor than the two described in the last chapter, as there is involved the principle of a trussed frame. The centre is formed of two frames like that shown, the face side at Fig. 10, and the reverse side at Fig. 11, consisting of four pieces each—namely,

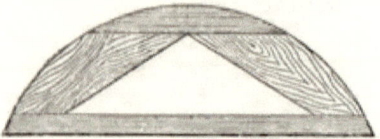

FIG. 11.—Elevation of Inside of Centre.

two principal bearers curved on edge to the required arc, and two tie pieces, one across the vertical joint directly under the crown and key brick to hold the bearers together, and a tie or foot piece to prevent the feet from slipping when weighted above. The binding cleats across the bottom and battens are as before described. To construct this frame, which is employed when the height of the arch to the soffit exceeds the width of an ordinary board, it is usual to describe the curve in the same way as before, using a rod or trammel on a drawing board or floor, and to mark the lines shown under the bevels as on Fig.

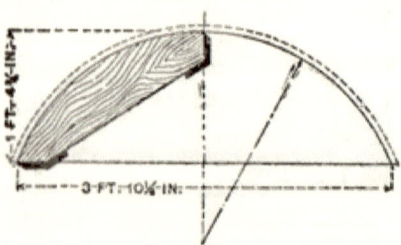

FIG. 12.—Method of obtaining Bevels.

12 in such a manner that the 1 in. board which is suitably wide enough can be applied, taking care that there will be enough stuff on to cut out the curve. Then by tacking this board to the floor, with its bottom edge to the indicated lines, the curve can be struck from the centre A, Fig. 12. Squaring up from the spring line and from the centre A, the plumb joint and bevel at the crown will be

found, likewise the foot bevels can be found on the spring line. Fig. 13 is a sketch of a board marked ready for sawing out the piece. Care must be taken to have the bevelled butt joints and curved edges perfectly square from the face, otherwise the whole construction will be twisted and unfit to sustain an arch whose soffit is intended to be level. Proceed to prepare the upper binding piece and

FIG. 13.—Half Curve of Frame.

lower tie, each about 3 in. wide and 1 in. thick, and to nail them on to the bearers after the manner of Figs. 10 and 11, using 8d. clinch nails, and turning their points when driven to insure a firm and stable frame; also dress off the upper piece to the curve of the bearers. Construct another similar frame to constitute a pair, and place them parallel to each other at a distance apart equal to the thickness of the intended arch, as shown at Fig. 14. Nail on

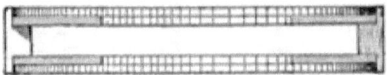

FIG. 14.—Plan of Frame Centre.

spaced battens and bottom cleats, as before illustrated, and the centre will be complete and ready for setting in position.

In order to set this centre four uprights will be necessary, one under each corner of the centre proper resting on thin double wedges placed on a block, as shown at Figs. 10 and 15. These are cut to the height of the spring line, less the thickness of cross-cleats, and are also toe-nailed to them. On the opposite faces of the uprights cross-blocks are affixed spanning the two uprights; between and against these blocks the required brace is tightly driven. By employing cross-blocks the necessity of using two braces is ob-

viated, with the same results, that is, pressing the uprights
firmly against the jambs by the braces acting on the blocks.
Should the lower ends of the uprights spring out by the pressure of the upper brace on their middle part another brace
can be placed, as indicated.   The construction of the centre
proper is more clearly shown in section at Fig. 15, repre-
senting as it does the brick rowlocks or rings constituting
the arch resting on the battens, the battens on the frames,

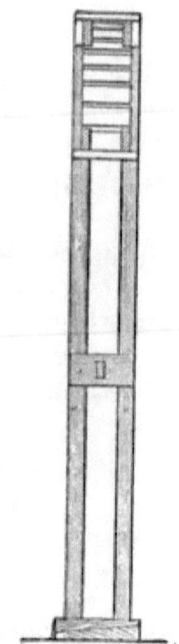

FIG. 15.—Section of Centre through Crown.

frames on cleats, cleats on uprights and uprights on wedges.
The object in using the latter under the uprights is to
gradually lower the centre by allowing it to fall by its own
weight from the superstructure above, so that the different
brick may come by degrees to their bearings without a too
sudden application of the weight exerted on the extrados
or upper side of the arch.   It is best to allow the centre to
remain some time in position, as removing it too soon en-
dangers the arch, which is never reliable until the mortar

is thoroughly set. Wedges, therefore, permit of convenient and early easing, yet still keep the work secure. Fig.
16 represents the centre for a semicircular arch of the same

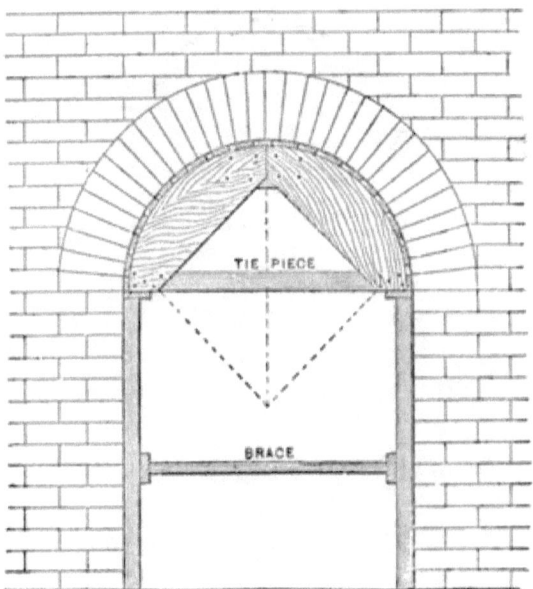

FIG. 16.—Centre of Horizontal Arch.

span and character as Fig. 10. It is similarly constructed,
excepting as regards the curved bearers, each of which
occupies a quadrant of one-half the semicircular curve,
Fig. 17. In connection with this it will be noticed that

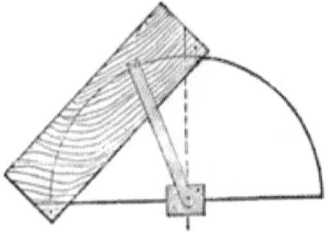

FIG. 17.—Striking the Curve.

when the centre is a part of a circle, a semicircle, a quadrant, etc., the bevels of the bearers will be equal. In this
case the bevel is an angle of 45°, as the bottom edges are

2

the two sides of a square. This is also the case with centres when the bottom edges form a semi-hexagon, semi-octagon, and so on with all polygon figures. In setting

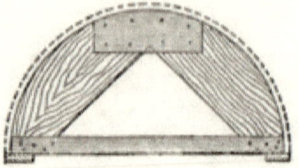

FIG. 18.—Elevation of Inside of Centre.

this centre the same process as has been just described is repeated, but if the opening be low the wedges can be omitted.

CHAPTER III.

SINCE the modern practice of centring is based on a well-tried system, it follows that simple centres employed in ordinary construction are similar in character, and are all planned in accordance with well-defined rules. The fact is plainly exemplified in Fig. 19 of the accompanying illustrations. In this a centre is constructed following the rules explained in the last chapter. It is made up of three principal bearers, the outer edges of which are curved to the required arc. The illustration also shows how a semicircular arch is subdivided into an equal number of parts, in which the bevels for the butt joints are always the same. It is not, however, always the case that the rough boards are of equal width. In many instances they are scrap stuff, so that the bevel shown in Fig. 20 cannot be applied. In such cases it is usual to lay out the curve and spring line, full size, on a floor. Divide the curved line into three equal spaces, as seen in Figs. 19 and 22, and draw lines to the centre point. By placing the rough boards over these lines, as indicated by the dotted section in Fig. 22, the bevel on the butt joints can be easily marked with a pencil or knife; then, by sawing on the mark, the joint will be obtained. The frame shown in Fig. 19 is stiffened by broad tie battens nailed across the beveled joints, as shown in Fig. 22 If the bearers be narrow, supporting braces must be nailed on the battens above and the tie piece running in the direction of the joint lines, to support the joint. Cross battens on the top edges of the curved

bearers may be ⅞ in. thick, or of any other convenient
thickness, but a thickness must be allowed for in striking
the curves.   The centre thus constructed is set up as before, placed on upright joists and wedges and sheathed in

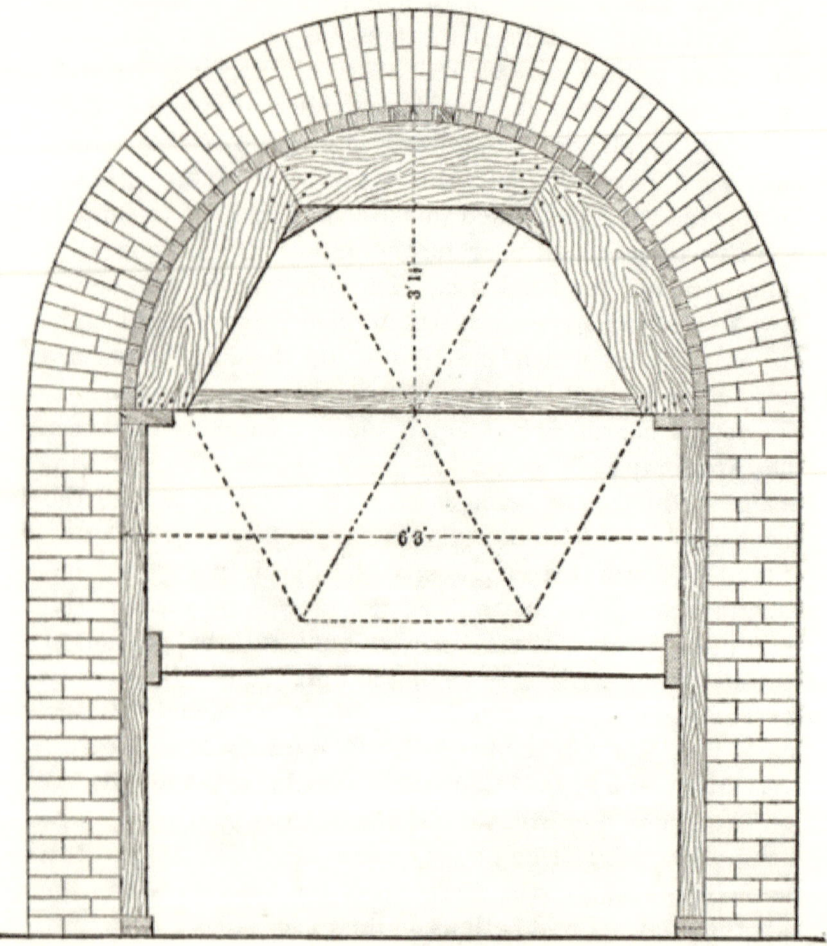

FIG. 19.—Wide Span, Semicircular Centre.

place between the jambs.   In cheap work it is not the rule
to employ wedges, but their use is obvious, and therefore
necessary for the purpose before stated.   In Fig. 23 another form of centre is shown, and one that involves more

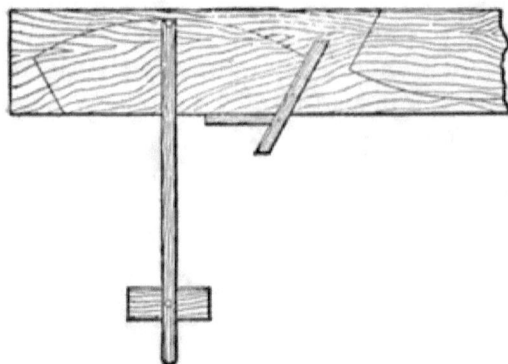

FIG. 20.—Striking out the Curves of the Bearers.

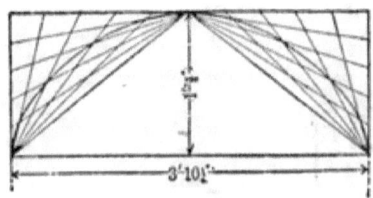

FIG. 21.—Elliptic Curve from Intersecting Lines.

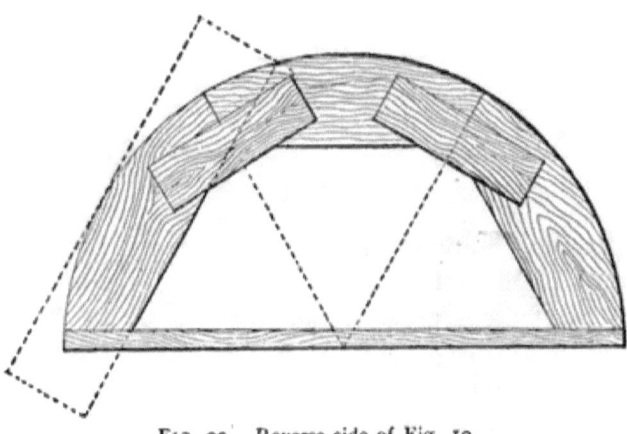

FIG. 22.— Reverse side of Fig. 19

skill and more careful consideration than anything we have
so far described. The centre is that which would be required in building an elliptical stone arch of 4 ft. span. The
plan of construction followed resembles that of the 4 ft. horizontal arch already referred to, but, inasmuch as the curve
is different, a different plan is followed, and getting curved

FIG. 23.—Elliptical Arch Centre.

bearers requires more labor. There are various methods
laid down in the books used by mechanics for sweeping
elliptical curves. A very desirable one for general use is
that indicated in Fig. 24. The illustration referred to
shows an elliptical curve struck by means of a sliding trammel. As this instrument is in daily use in all shops of any
pretensions throughout the country, it is well known, and

therefore requires very brief description. It consists of two ⅞ × 2 in. grooved cross pieces halved together. Slides are provided in which pins are inserted. To these pins a trammel rod is fixed which works at the required distance necessary to trace the curve. The trammel is set here as in all cases—that is to say, the distance from the lower pin to the tracer is equal to half of the long diameter—in other words, the spring line or major axis of the elliptical arch. The distance from the upper pin to the tracer is equal to half the short diameter of the elliptic arch or its rise. The curve shown is for the bearers in Fig. 24, one of which is

FIG. 24.—Striking an Elliptic Curve with Trammel.

shown in the left-hand part of the sketch. Of course, the centre lines marked on the ends of the trammel are placed directly on the centre lines of the draft board; it is there tacked fast.

Fig. 21 illustrates another common method of striking an elliptical curve. It is the method commonly known as intersection of lines. It is not nearly so desirable for use in practical work as the one illustrated in Fig. 24. The same mode of construction and setting as was used in the horizontal arch is employed in this case.

Since arches of wide span necessitate large voussoirs to resist the strain acting on their extrados, or upper side, wide spans call for larger centres and strong, reliable con- .

struction.   The elliptical span gateway shown in Fig. 27
illustrates this.   Owing to the size and shape of the stones
employed in this work, considerable weight rests on the
centre used for the purpose.   There is also another feature
connected with this centre which must be considered and
allowed for.   The key-stone projects 1 in. below the face

FIG. 25.—Reverse side of Fig. 27.

of the soffit.   The centre is therefore built in a way to
make allowance for this.   On a clean, level floor the spring
line is drawn, as shown in Fig. 26.   Having an arch of 10
ft. span, this line would be run, probably, 12 ft. long.
A centre point is established from which a line is drawn,
square up, extending to the height of the rise of the frame,
in this case 1 ft. 5 in.   The line is continued below the

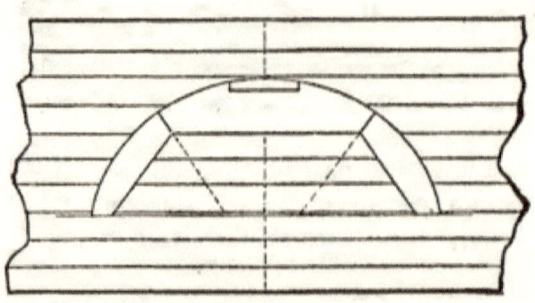

FIG. 26.—Laying down an Elliptical Frame.

spring line, as indicated.   The trammel is then set as already described, and the elliptical curve drawn.   To find
the bevelled joints we divide the curve into four equal
parts, and mark on the spring line the distance from the
spring point to the first division.   We join these by a
straight line, which gives us the direction of the bevel
joints.   Place the rough boards, out of which the centre is

to be made, so that they will be wide enough to cut the
curve and mark them out, as shown in the illustration.
Cut out of the middle piece a notch for the key-stone,
measuring the width on each side of the vertical centre line.
This frame, like the one shown in Fig. 19, is stiffened by
battens resting on two braces, as in Fig. 22.   The number
of the pieces is as follows: Curved bearers 1 ½ in. thick by
12 in. wide, tie-piece 2 × 6 in., battens across joints 1 ½ × 8

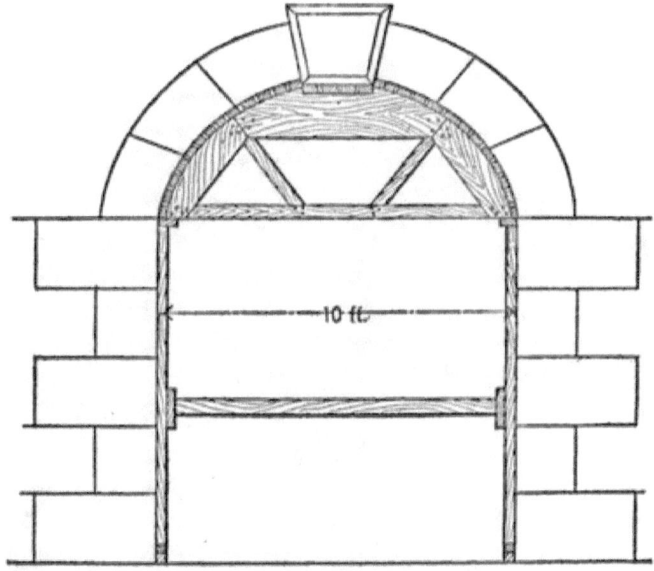

FIG. 27.—Centre for an Elliptical Gateway.

in., supporting braces 2 × 4 in.; the whole is firmly spiked
together with 20d. spikes.   The top of the centre is covered
with 1 in. cleats, spaced ½ in. apart.   The bottom cleats
are 2 × 4 in., the uprights 3 × 6 in.; and the shore between
the beams 3 × 6 in.   Great care must be exercised in setting
a centre for stone work, since different stones are worked
exactly to their shape and size, and the centre must be
perfectly true, so that the joints will come right.

CHAPTER IV.

CONTINUING the general subject of Centring, several illustrations of which are presented herewith, I would first direct attention to Fig. 28, which shows very plainly the necessity of using great care and accuracy in setting centres in order to carry stone work. Here the voussoirs are cut to correspond with the running courses of ashlar, and are bound into the wall, thereby insuring great stability. The arch, 16 ft. in diameter, is sustained by a framed centre constructed on the Howe principle, the whole construction being placed in tension and tightened by the iron bolt. The bolt A is headed at the top and passes through the transverse piece B, the foot of the brace and tie-piece C bringing the weight on the bearer joints D D entirely on the centre of the longitudinal tie-piece E'. This is suspended on A passing through B. B is supported by the braces F F, which rest on the tie-piece E. The weight, being carried on the uprights, rests solidly on the stone sill below. On the lower side of the tie-piece is shown how the bearer joints are all similar, the inside figure being an octagon and the bevels G G being set to the same angle. The curve of the centre is carried below the centre line or diameter. This is done for architectural effect; hence, the spring line must be indicated and the bearers must be laid out from it; all lines below must be drawn parallel to it. The timber used in the construction of centres of large diameter must be sound in character and of large dimensions.   The tie-piece in this case is 2×8 in., braced with 2×8 in., halved together in crossing, and joggled into the tie-piece.   The braces should not be less than 1½ in. thick, and should be as wide as possible.   The bearers should be 2 in. thick; the transverse piece B should be 3×6 in.; the wrought-iron rod should be 1 in. in diameter.   Since the stones weigh a

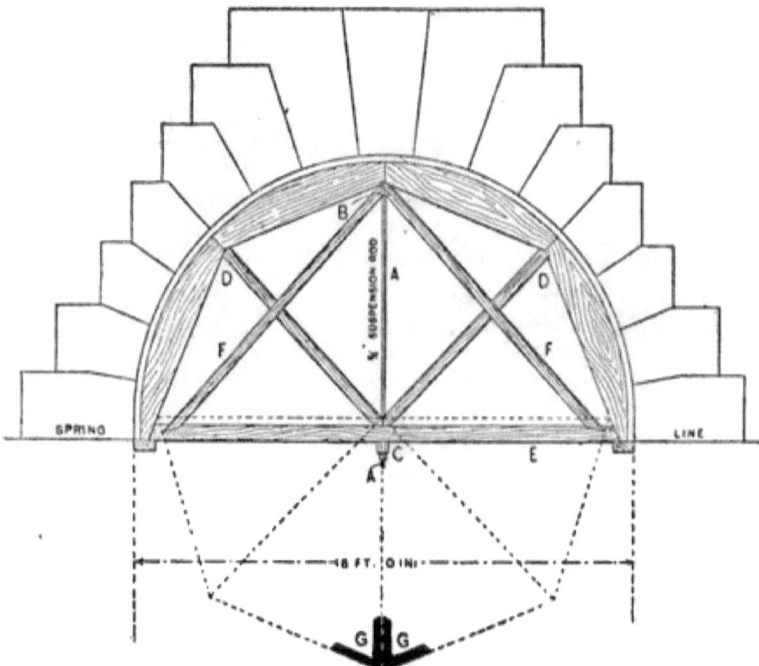

FIG. 28.—Large Centre in Ashlar Work.

considerable amount, the centre must be strong enough to support them without risk.   This design of arch, which has a leaning to the Moorish or horseshoe pattern, is greater than a semicircle, and was used in a large building in Brooklyn, N. Y., some time since.   In this case the centre was carried on the projecting imposts of the capitals.

The centres of Gothic arches are many and varied in form; but they are easily struck, however, from the central point or radii shown by architects in their detail drawings.

The simplest to strike out is the equilateral arch centre, shown in Fig. 29. The centres for striking the curves are

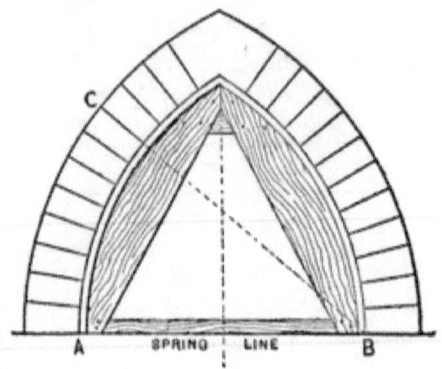

FIG. 29.—Equilateral Arch.

plainly indicated. The head or rise of the arch is equal to the span or width. From this it will be seen that straight lines joining the apex with the base will form an equilateral

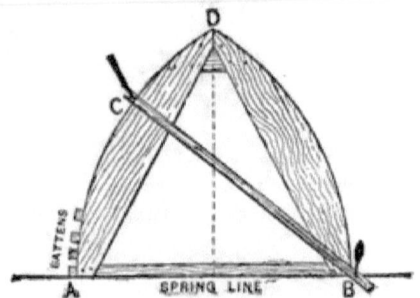

FIG. 30.—Laying out the Bearers for a Gothic Arch.

triangle. The centres for striking out the curves for bearers, therefore, will be on the base or spring line, as A and B.

FIG. 31.—Plan of Centre.

B C in Fig. 30 is a rod striking the left curve. From A to the apex D all stone or brick joints run in the direction of

C B.   Fig. 31 is a plan of the centre without the apex ties, showing the edges of the bearers and lower tie-pieces.

The obtuse point or drop arch illustrated in Fig. 32 is

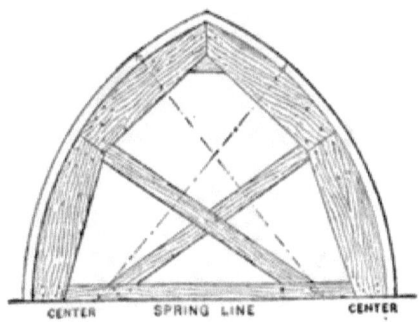

FIG. 32.—Centre for a Drop Arch.

constructed from centres on the base line.   The radius is less than the span.   It will be easily understood from the preceding description.   All braces, however, must, as is shown, run in the direction of the centres, from which the

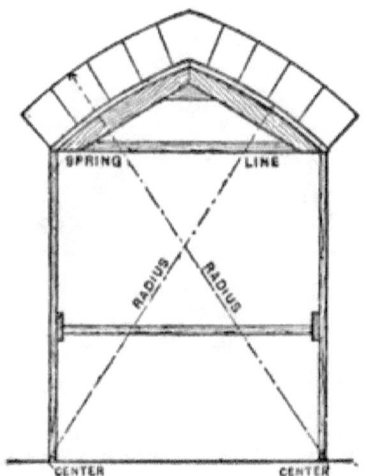

FIG. 33.—Another form of Drop Arch.

curves are struck.   This arch is supposed to be 6 ft. in span.   Fig. 33 illustrates another arch of the same character, the radii of which run to centres far below the spring

line, being on the jamb line and drawn square to the spring
line.   The lancet Gothic arch, Fig. 34, has striking centres, which are likewise on the spring line, but differs from
those described last in the radius being longer than the
width of the span.   The lines join in a way to form an
isosceles triangle, the height of which is greater than the
width.   For large centres, calling for long bearers, the
method followed in the sketch is the best, having, if such

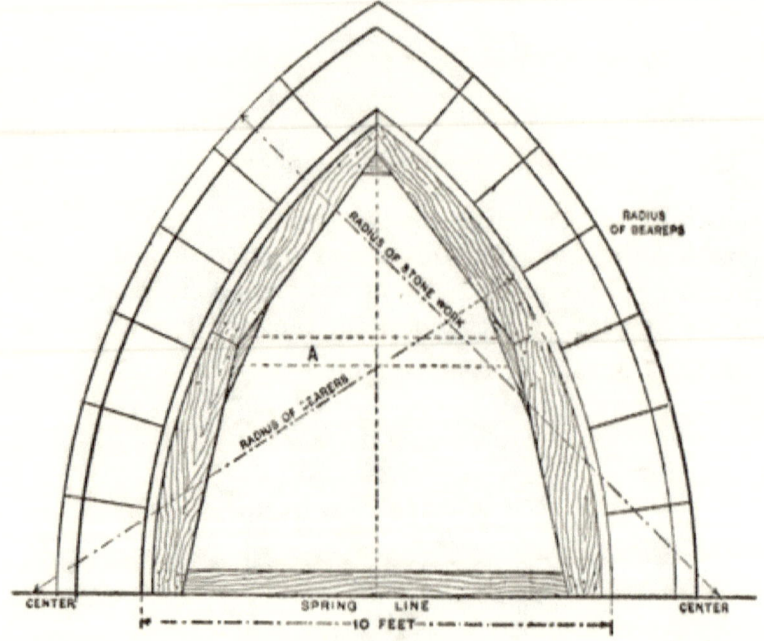

FIG. 34.—Lancet Gothic Arch.

is needed, the extra brace shown by the dotted lines.   This
should be inserted and nailed to the joint tie-piece.   Small
centre bearers, of course, can be cut out of one piece of
board, as already described.   Joints, lines and braces must
run on radial lines.

Tudor arches vary much in shape, and are all struck
from centres within the arch.   The arch represented at
Fig. 35 is struck from four centres, two of which are on the
spring line, and formed by dividing the spring line into

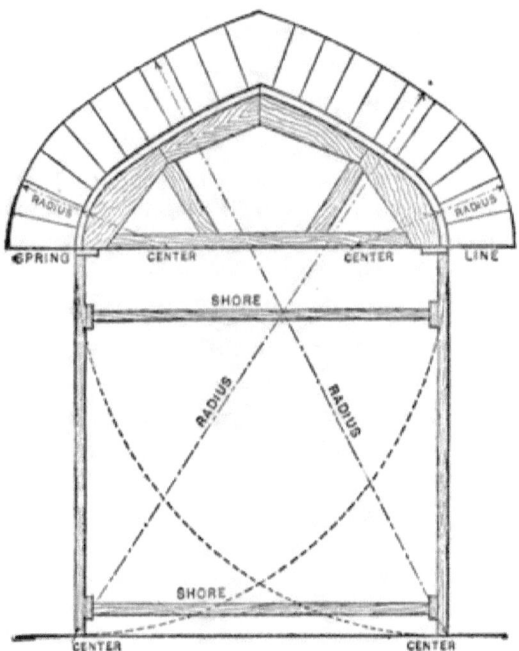

FIG. 35.—Centers for a Four Centre Arch.

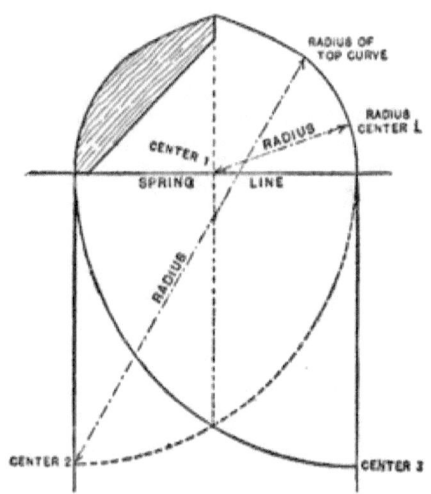

FIG. 36.—Diagram of a Three Centre Arch.

four equal parts, the two outside divisions indicating the
radii required for the lower curves. The centres for the
upper curves are found by taking the whole width of the
span as radius and cutting the line of the jamb with this
radius, as shown in Fig. 35. The intersection will be the
centre desired, and the radius will be to the tangential
point of the small curve. However, as centres are usually
given by the architects to strike out all arches, the above
will be sufficient to aid the beginner when he meets this
arch. It will be noticed that as the joint of the curve
bearers is above the tangential point, so all braces must run
to the centres for the upper curves. Fig. 36 is a three-
centre arch, showing one bearer, the striking-out points,
and radii.

CHAPTER V

CENTRING CIRCULAR WINDOWS.

THE frequent occurrence of circular windows in the façades of ecclesiastical edifices often causes contractors some difficulty in erecting temporary centres to sustain the voussoirs above the spring line until the bond is complete. A comparatively simple method is shown in the illustration, based on the chordal system, and consists of the usual centre proper and its supporting auxiliaries. The peripheral truss of the centre is constructed on the old principle of pieces sawed to the sweep abutting together in joints whose planes are in the direction of the radii of the centre of the circle, the joints being secured by similar pieces across the back, breaking joint. This construction is held together by a tie-piece, the bottom edge of which is supported at the radial joints by struts directed from the centre of the circle, the whole being firmly nailed together. Two of these frames are employed, placed equidistant from each other, equal to the thickness of the stone facing. On the edges of the periphery the battens or pieces which form a smooth surface on which to lay the voussoirs are affixed, and two cleats, as shown, are fastened across the lower edges of the tie-pieces. This operation gives a strong, safe centre for arches up to 15 ft. in diameter. The dimensions of the pieces are as follows: Pieces on periphery, $1\frac{1}{2} \times 8$ in.; tie-pieces, $1\frac{1}{2} \times 8$ in.; struts, $1\frac{1}{2} \times 3$ in.; battens, $1\frac{1}{4} \times 2$ in. The supports are few in number and cut in as represented. The bottom piece (in compression) is placed level, bearing on the intrados at the points A and B. From these points pieces reach to the cleats, C and D, and at the spring line hold the centre proper in its posi-

3

tion. From the point A, also resting on the joint A, the
tie-piece A E, parallel to B D, supports the centre of the
tie-piece which receives the thrusts of the braces above.
Similarly B F, parallel to A C, sustains a like strain, both

FIG. 37.—Centring for Circular Window.

pieces abutting against the bolster, E F. The vertical
piece shown can be inserted if it be necessary for additional
security, and the sustaining pieces can either be of two sets
—that is, one under each separate truss—or if the wall be
only a facing of moderate thickness, one will be sufficient.

CHAPTER VI

SUSPENDED CENTRES.

THE following existing method of forming temporary supports and centres in the construction of fire-proof floors may prove useful. The first example, Fig. 38, shows a terra-cotta floor, after being laid between two

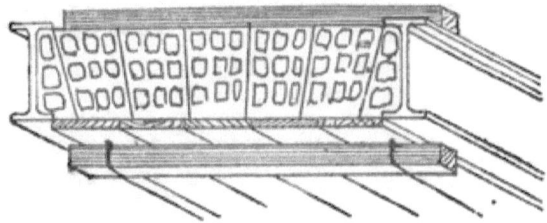

FIG. 38.—Terra-Cotta Arching on Suspended Planking.

beams. As will be noticed, it rests on a staging of 1½ in. mason's plank, resting on a 4 × 4 in. joist, which is supported by a ⅝ in. iron hook, which has on the upper end a screw thread and nut. This hook is made like Fig. 39. The

FIG. 39.—Hanger for Carrying Suspended Joist.

hook passes through the 1½ in. plank and through another 4 × 4 in. joist, which rests across the top side of the beam, and is bored out to allow it to pass through, from which the staging is suspended and held securely by the nuts and washers. Three or more of those are used as is necessary, according to the size of the floor. The utility of this

FIG. 40.—Centre for Small Arches.

method is apparent, as it leaves the floor or space underneath perfectly free from incumbrance, and the temporary staging can be more safely lowered, thereby providing against accidents in case the terra-cotta should not be sufficiently bonded and drop down. The hooks used generally are of ⅝ or ¾ in. round iron, long enough to suit the depth of the beams, plus the thickness of the joints, and a

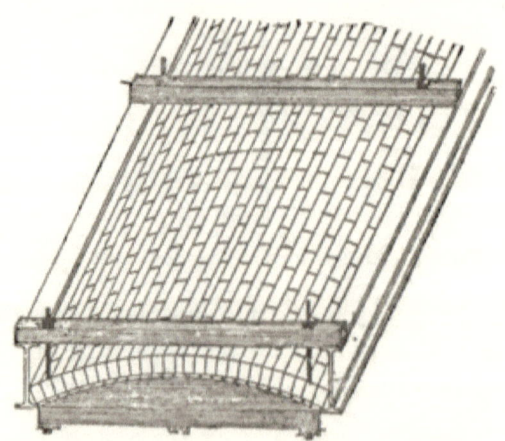

FIG. 41.—Arch Turned on Suspended Centres.

brick is generally left out where the hook passes through.

Fig. 40 represents the way in which masons temporarily support their arched brick floors; in this case an arch of small space. The drawing shows the ordinary form of timber centre hung from a joist across the top side of the beam by bolts, which pass through another joist on the bottom side of the centre which rests on it. These centres are generally made from five to eight feet in length, according to convenience, and are moved along as section after section is completed. They can be lowered in a similar manner to Fig. 38, with the nuts on the top edges of the upper joists.

In Fig. 41 the projection of a brick arch turned on its

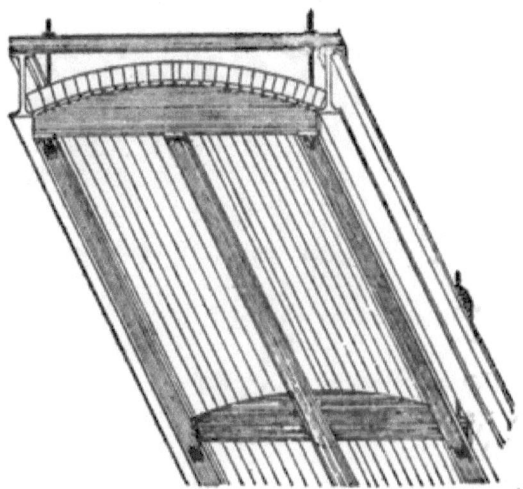

FIG. 42.—Bottom View of Centre, Showing its Position between Girders.

necessary centre is seen with suspending joist and the lowering nuts. The centre differs from the others in not having any bottom joist, but merely a bottom 2 in. strip, tying the frame together, through which the bolts pass, each bolt being close to each frame, as in Fig. 42. The frames in these centres are spaced comparatively close together, to support the dead weight above them when laying the brick.

CHAPTER VII.

IN order to make a skew centre it will be necessary to first explain to the reader what a skew arch really is. Mr. Peter Nicholson, in his " Encyclopedia of Architecture," defines it as "an arch the face of which stands obliquely with reference to the inner faces of the piers." He likewise states that " the first skew arch was built across the Mugone River, at Florence, Italy, A. D. 1550."

From Mr. E. Dobson's useful little book, "The Art of Building," we take the following: "The skew arch is one in which it is not possible to lay the courses parallel to the abutments; for were this done, the thrust being at right angles to the direction of the courses, a great portion of the arch on each side would have nothing to keep it from falling. In order to bring the thrust into the right direction, the courses must therefore be laid as nearly as possible at right angles to the fronts of the arch and at an angle with the abutments, and it is this which produces the skew or oblique arch."

The statics or construction of the masonry of the arch proper is, however, slightly apart from this book, which is written to explain to carpenters the proper method to follow in building the centre necessary to turn the arch. We think our readers will find it instructive and useful in practice. Fig. 43 represents the constructed centre looking down from above, and shows it complete and ready for setting in position, *a a, b b, c c* and *d d* being the main frames, constructed in the manner shown at A, Fig. 44, which is simple in form and still strong and fit. As the arch penetrates the wall at an angle of 45 degrees, it fol-

lows that the shape of the front elevation or face will be a
regular ellipse, as shown in outline over *e* F, Fig. 44.
This curve is found by dividing the circumference of the
semicircular frame, *e e e*, into any number of equal divisions,
then transferring these divisions by ordinates drawn perpendicular to the spring line, cutting the diagonal seat of
the elliptic elevation *e* F, Fig. 44. From these points, by
raising up perpendiculars to *e* F and making them equal in
height to those at *e e e*, points will then be found through
which the exact curve of the elevation can be traced. A
frame must be made to this curve, and have its edge bevelled to the angle of 45 degrees on the plan, as shown on

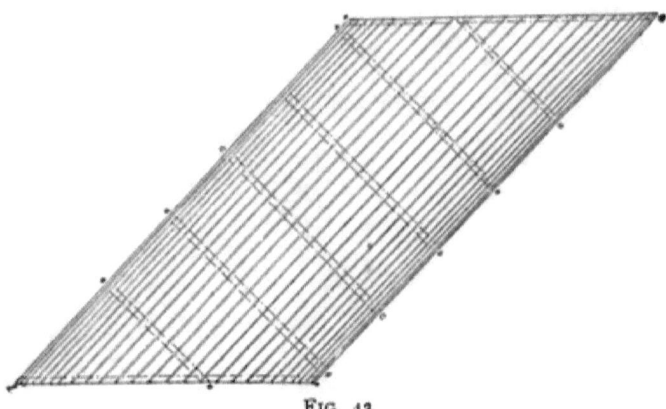

FIG. 43.

the right side at Fig. 45, so that the battens will fit close
to arris formed by the face and top edge of the frame, which
will be placed as *e* F, Figs. 43 and 44. There will also be
two half frames or bearers required like Fig. 46, one at
each end, which are to have their upper ends sawn to a
mitre or angle of 45 degrees, to fit against the inside face
of the elevation frame, *e* F, and be securely nailed to it
square with the sides *e* F. To put this centre together, lay
the longitudinal stringer bearers, P P, Fig. 45, down on
the floor and tack on each frame in its position, as shown
by the dotted lines at Fig. 43, and then after bracing the
whole construction square, by squaring the bearers, *e* F,
Fig. 43, with the frames, *a a*, *b b*, *c c*, *d d*, nail the battens

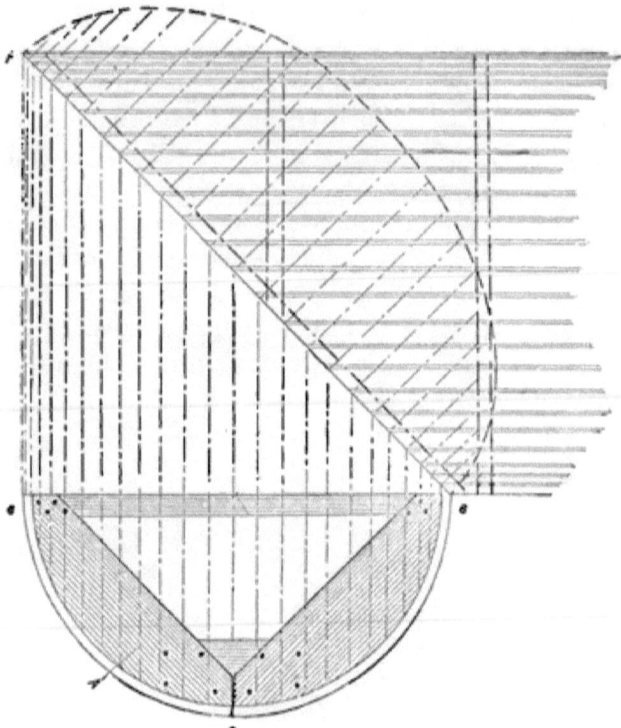

FIG. 44.

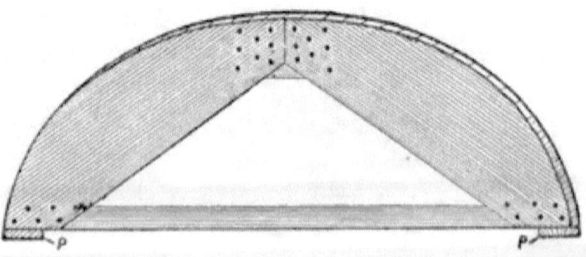

FIG. 45.

round till they are all on. Afterwards saw off the projecting ends flush with the faces of the front frames. The
skew centre must now be turned up and the stringer bearers
nailed on solid, and the centre is ready for setting. Great
care must be exercised in setting this form of centre in or-

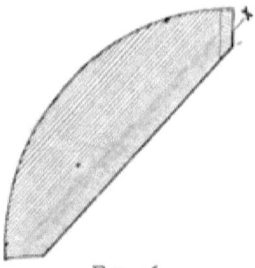

FIG. 46.

der that it may be perfectly level at the spring line and
across on the stringer bearers. It should be set on good
uprights resting on oak wedges of slight taper and be well
braced, to be conveniently eased, immovable and not likely
to be jarred out of its proper position. This is important
to a good result.

CHAPTER VIII.

THE essential appliances, termed centres, though usually of a simple character, ofttimes assume uncommon forms, and in this chapter we place before our readers something which the majority are likely to be unfamiliar with. They occur generally in the construction of ecclesiastical or public buildings, and, as the art of building frequently forces carpenters and builders to use knowledge outside of routine practice, it will be wise for our readers to be familiar with their construction in case they require it. Building is a progressive art, and we can say from experience that it is always best to keep ahead in the matter of information, in order that there may be no possibility of ever being retarded by a difficulty.

Flaring or splayed centres are those that open or spread outward, and are used to form or turn splayed arches whose soffits also flare or widen to the front. These are the outcome of the use of very thick walls, and were largely introduced by the mediæval builders for the purpose of spreading the light to either side, which would be impossible were the splayed sides omitted; also for lessening the apparent great thickness of the walls. When the jambs were thus moulded it necessarily followed that the soffit of the arch should be similarly treated, and it is to explain how the centres for turning them were constructed that this article was written. That the mediæval builders employed them cannot for a moment be doubted, and it is not meet that we of the nineteenth century should be deficient in any knowledge which our predecessors wielded to so much advantage.

Reference to Fig. 47 of the illustrations shows a centre for a splayed semicircular arch of 4 ft. span, with a splay of

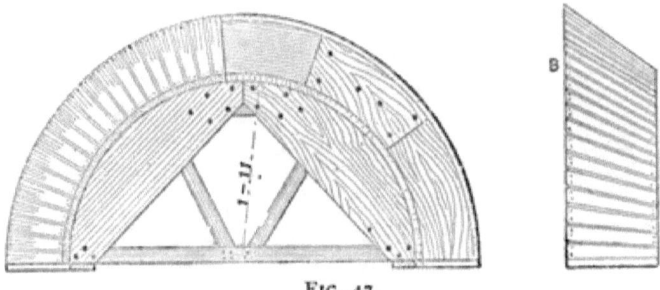

FIG. 47.

8 in. in 12 in. depth of jamb, which will be seen by measuring the side view of the completed centre drawn to the right. This centre, like all the others previously described, will

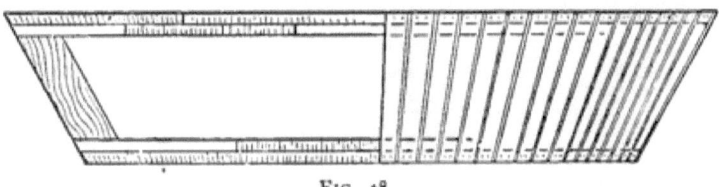

FIG. 48.

require two frames, as A and B, Figs. 47 and 48, each of which will be of a different diameter and struck from a different radii; that is, the smaller frame will have

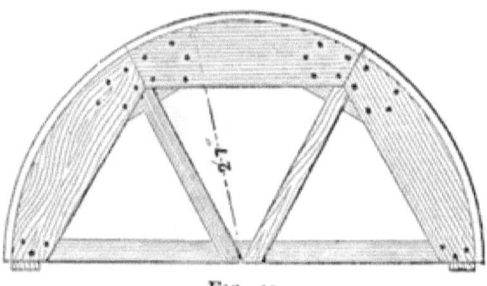

FIG. 49.

its edge made to a curve struck with a 1 ft. 11 in. radius, and with the larger struck with a 2 ft. 7 in. radius. The edges of these frames must be bevelled all round to

the splay shown on the side view, in order that the battens
will fit closely to them and make the necessary angle to

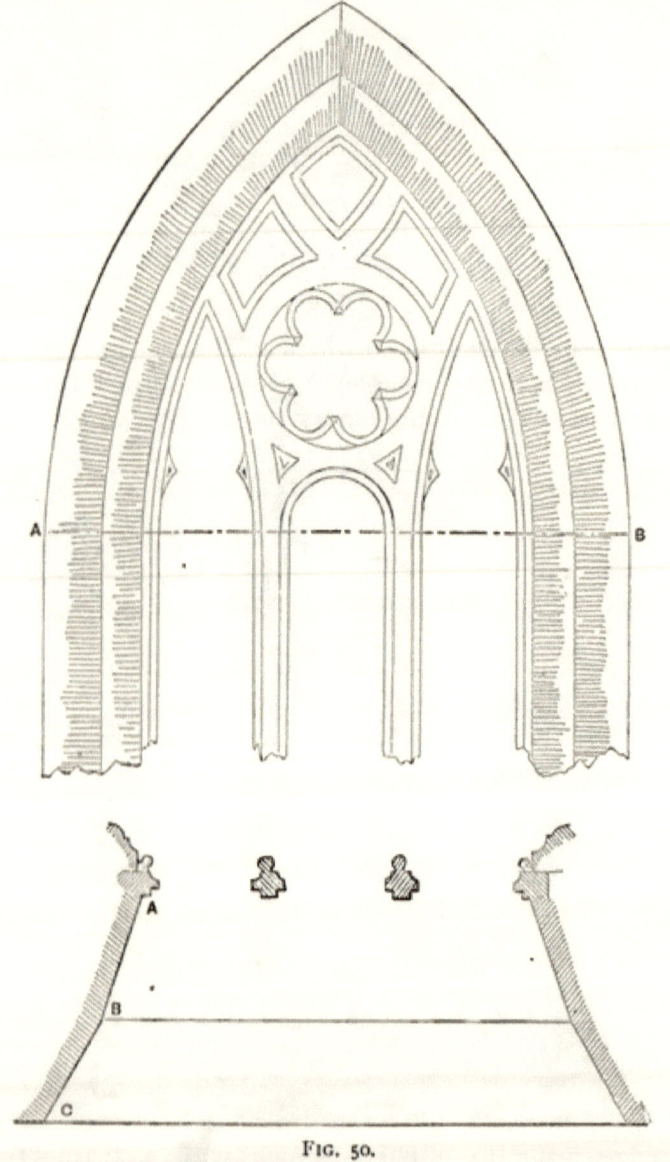

FIG. 50.

which the arch will be turned. . The reader will understand
this better by looking at the right side of the sketch (Fig.

47) at the elevation of the frames where the bevelled edges
are shown, only one-half of them being covered with battens. The plan of the centre, Fig. 48, also shows this
more distinctly, and also the bevels of the frames wrought
to the angle of the splay. Carpenters will require to exer-
cise a little more care in constructing this form of centre
than is usually done, as it is for a special purpose. Fig. 49
is the elevation of the large frame, and is slightly different
in construction from the smaller. Fig. 50 is the elevation
of a Gothic window having jambs and soffit with a double
flare or splay, which is done to break the excessive depth

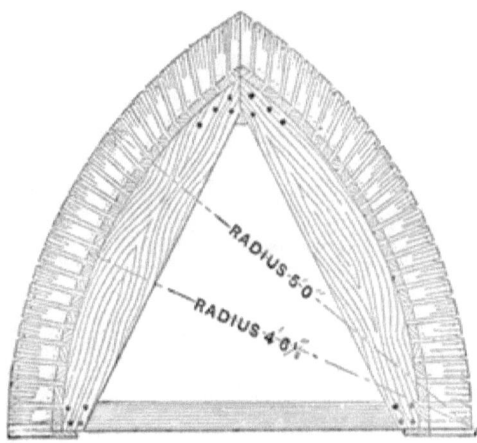

FIG. 51.

of surface consequent on a thick wall. As the plan shows,
two centres, which flare at different angles, will be needed
here, or one centre with two flares of unequal angles. The
first method is the best, however; that is, to make two
separate centres and bolt them together so they will fit at
the spring line, A B, in the manner necessary to enable the
mason to properly turn his arch. There is very little difference between this appliance and the one described above,
that is, taking each centre singly, but as there is a double
splay, then there must be a double centre in order to turn
the arch. One may be seen by referring to Fig. 51 of the
illustrations, and the reader will have no difficulty, from

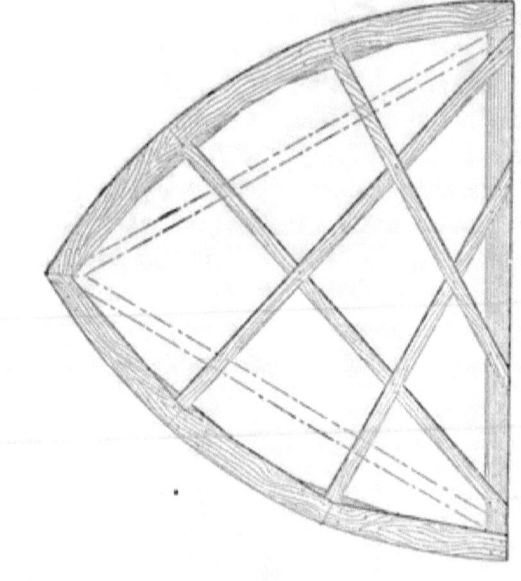

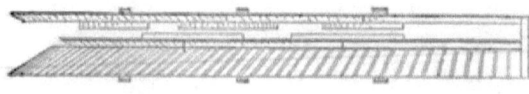

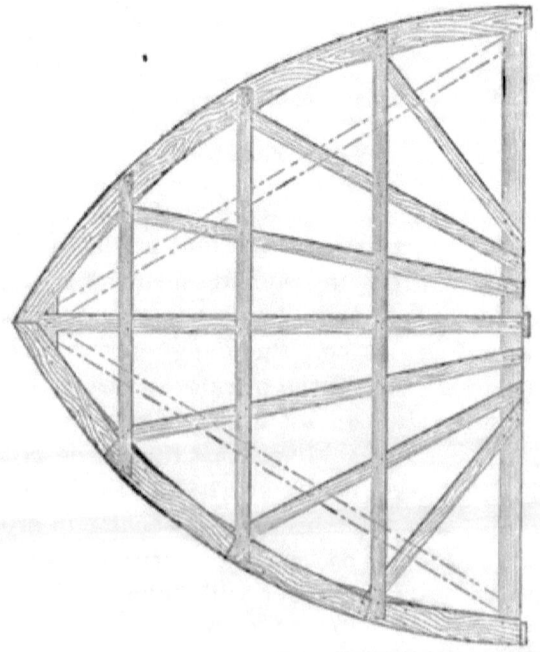

FIG. 52.

what has already been said, in making a centre of this
kind.

In connection with this subject our readers will doubtless
meet some very unique modes of applying it.   One which
has come to my notice is that which Mr. James Renwick,
the senior member of the firm of Renwick, Aspinwall &
Russell, of New York, introduced into the new Church of
All Saints, at 129th Street and Madison Avenue, New York
City.   Here it is placed in many ways, as at Figs. 50 and 51 ;
also in a window-opening embracing twin Gothic windows
which had splayed jambs, as A B, Fig. 50, and on the inside wall they were spanned by a four-centre arch forming
a recess of another flare, as B C, Fig. 50, which made up the
full thickness of the wall.   Another way in which it was
used was that represented at Fig. 52. ' This form of centre
was employed in turning the arches of the arcades dividing
the nave and right and left aisles.   It was adopted because
the soffits of the arches were built V-shaped in order that
plaster mouldings might be readily run on them.   The
whole construction was as described before, and made up of
two centres of the same splay, which were bolted together
in the manner shown in the side view drawn in the centre
of Fig. 52, where, to the left, is shown the battens covering
the frames, and, to the right, the exposed frames before
the battens are nailed on.   On account of the large sweep
of the curves of the arch (which was about 15 ft. span) and
the necessity for economizing material and labor, the carpenter was compelled to use sound judgment in framing
his centre, that it might be sufficiently strong to sustain the
superincumbent weight; so a trussing system was followed
in constructing it.

CHAPTER IX.

TWO EXAMPLES OF CENTRES SUITABLE FOR WIDE SPANS.

A S the centring of arches is a detail of builders' practice
which is continually involving special forms of con-
structive carpentry to sustain the superincumbent weight
placed on the centre, I deem it advisable to place before
the reader two principles of construction which are excel-
lent.   The first, Fig. 53, was used in the new office build-

FIG. 53.—Centre for Semi-circular Arch of 20 ft. Span.

ing recently erected by Messrs. Jackson & Co., of Union
Square, in New York.   As will be noticed, it was entirely

constructed without bolts or any ironwork of any kind excepting the nails necessary to hold the framed joints together. The trussing was most economically done, and the timbers kept uninjured. At the same time the heavy stone forming the ring of the arch were ably carried. This centre was 20 ft. span and carried a 24 in. wall. The centre for the segmental arch, illustrated at Fig. 54, is a trussed form, which might be followed with safety; but a still better method would be to carry the feet of the braces over to the suspension rods on the chord. In concluding this interesting subject I would recommend those who have occasion to use centres to always be on the safe side and make their construction more than strong enough, for there are very many cases recorded in the history of building construction where insufficient or improper centring has caused the failure of valuable works.

4

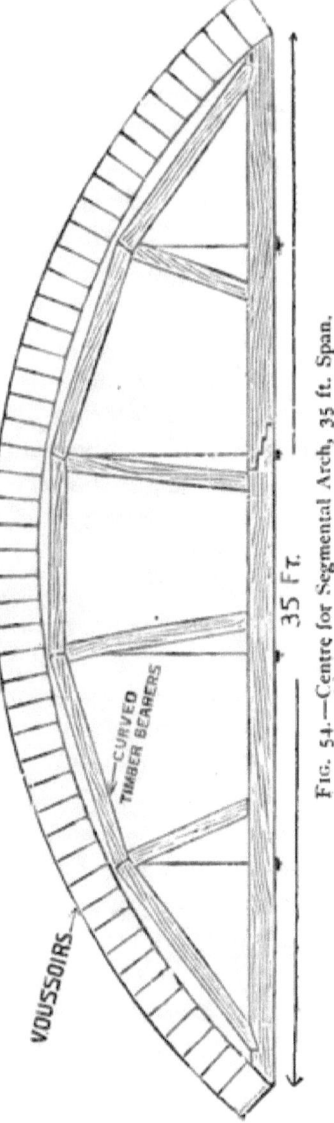

FIG. 54.—Centre for Segmental Arch, 35 ft. Span.

CHAPTER X.

THE centres previously described are those mostly used in the construction of buildings, but these appliances are also requisite in the construction of subterranean structures, such as sewers. It is for the purpose of showing the carpenter how to make them correctly that this form of centre is now described. Ordinary brick sewers are generally built in two ways—of cylindrical and of egg-shaped sections; that is, in the ordinary sewers used in general street work throughout the country. As the section of a sewer cut through at right angles is comparatively familiar to all carpenters, it would seem almost unnecessary to reproduce it here; still the writer thinks it safer to show how the centre used in turning the arch is made and set.

Fig. 55 of the illustrations represents the cross section (cut at right angles to the direction of its length) of a circular or cylindrical sewer whose diameter or bore is 2 ft., with the lower part or *invert* and the upper part or *arch* turned on the centre required. To build the invert to the shape shown, the mason works and guides the construction by moulds or templates put together after the manner of the frames described before, using two, and stretching lines from one to the other to guide the courses of brickwork as he goes along. He usually builds a sewer in lengths or sections of six, eight or ten feet at a time. When the lower course is built up to a height of one course of brick above the spring line, as shown in the illustration, Fig. 55, the centre is set in the manner as drawn here, resting on three pieces of 2 ×4 in. stud stuff placed under each end of the centre proper. This centre, unlike those described hereto-

fore, is made in a long length measuring 6, 8 or 10 ft., so
that the arch covers what has been built of the lower part.
It will be noticed that the centre is set about 2½ in. above the
spring line, which is done so it may be handily lowered and
slid out, thus making it available for the next length of
sewer.   It will likewise be noticed that the supporting
uprights are all loose, so that they may be readily knocked
away to permit the centre to drop down to the spring line
or widest part of the cylindrical bore, and by this means
loosening it and allowing it to slide freely out.   Readers

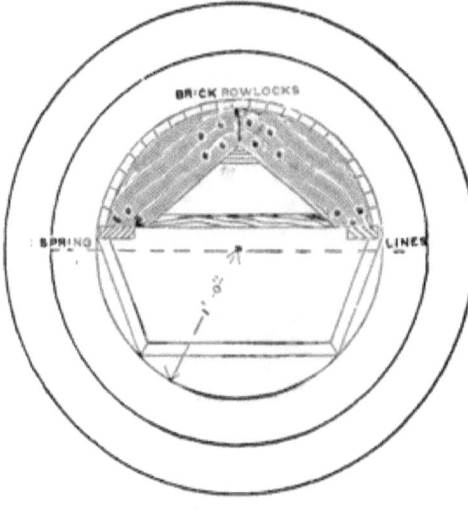

FIG. 55.

will readily comprehend that it would be impossible to ease
the centre were it set at the spring line in the manner of
wall centres.
    Carrying the subject further along, the egg-shaped form
is shown at Fig. 56, where the constructed sewer is drawn
in isometrical projection, part of the brickwork being left
off to give the reader a clearer idea as to how the centre
is placed above the spring line. The bottom portion is, as in
the case of the last, built from a template which is made by
the carpenter.   In order to make this template to the
proper shape, it must be laid out by a geometrical process

to the outline shown on the engineer's drawings, so it
would be well for the reader to thoroughly understand how
this is done. Fig. 57 explains the method by which egg-
shapes are laid down.   A B is a centre line or plumb line,
and C D any other line drawn at right angles to it.   With

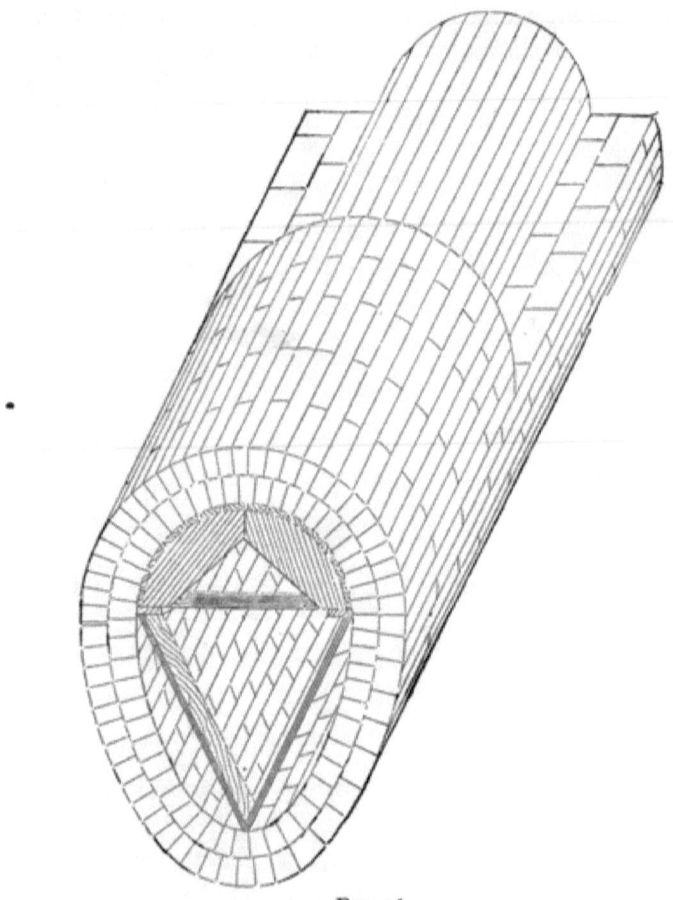

FIG. 56.

the intersection of the lines as centre and 12 in. radius strike
the semicircle C A D.   Produce C D to E F and make C E
and D F equal to C G.   Now make G B equal to C D, and
divide B G into four equal divisions.   Next take H as
centre and H B as radius and describe the circle shown.

From E and F as centres, with E D and F C as radii, strike arcs, joining the smaller bottom circle with the larger, C A D, which will complete the figure. The template to be

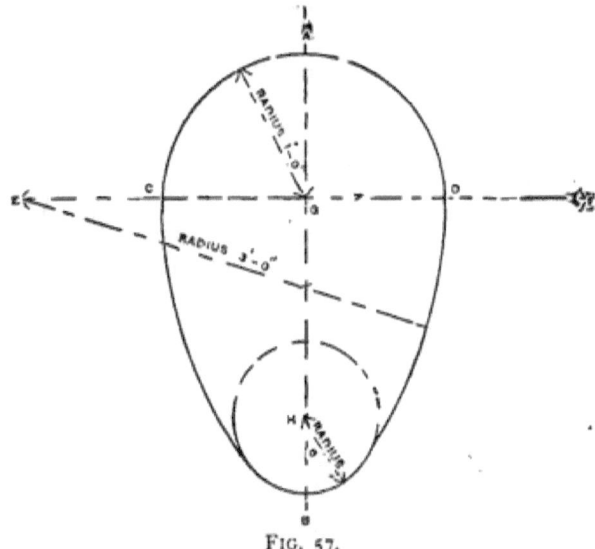

FIG. 57.

made to the outline C B D is represented at Fig. 58, where the method of putting it together is exemplified. This figure should be laid out on a drawing board or floor, and the

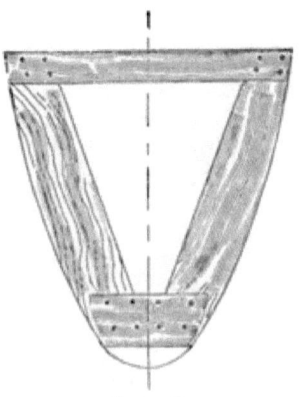

FIG. 58.

two side pieces marked and sawn to the outline of the bottom portion of the egg-shape. The centre necessary for

the arch is made as described above, and for a sewer of
these dimensions might have the parts of the following
sizes: Stuff to be rough spruce or pine strongly nailed
together; frames 1½ in. thick, battens 1 in. or 1¼ in. thick,
supporting uprights 2 ×4 in.   In connection with this subject of sewer centres a very peculiar feature is shown at Fig.
59.   It is the plan or top view of a centre forming the con-
tinuation of the arch from one street to another, or, prop-

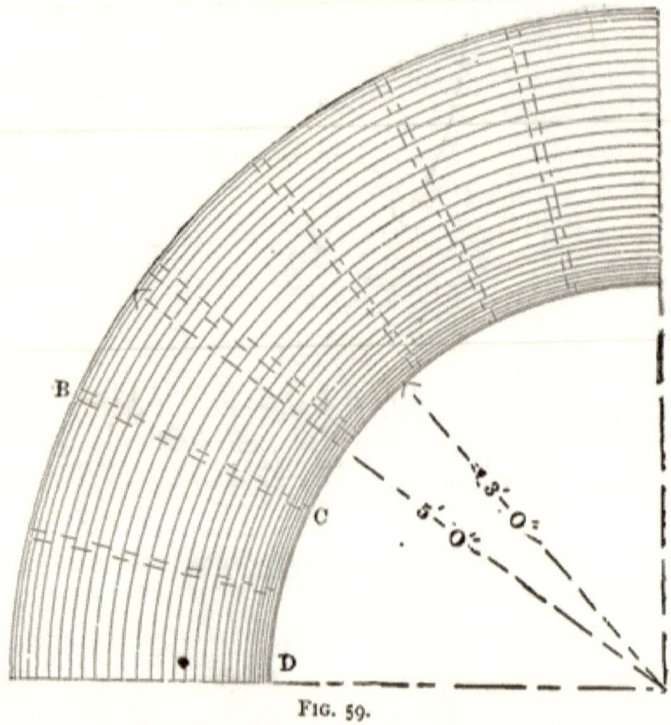

FIG. 59.

erly, a rectangled bend in the sewer.   In building this the
carpenter will make the frames or bearers radiate to a common centre, as Fig. 59, and be obliged to cut the battens
to a curve the shape of which can be determined by the
following process: Let A B C D, Fig. 60, be the plan of
the annular or ring vault to be turned.   It is required to
find the shape of the covering boards or battens which will
be nailed on the frames.   The edges of the frames being

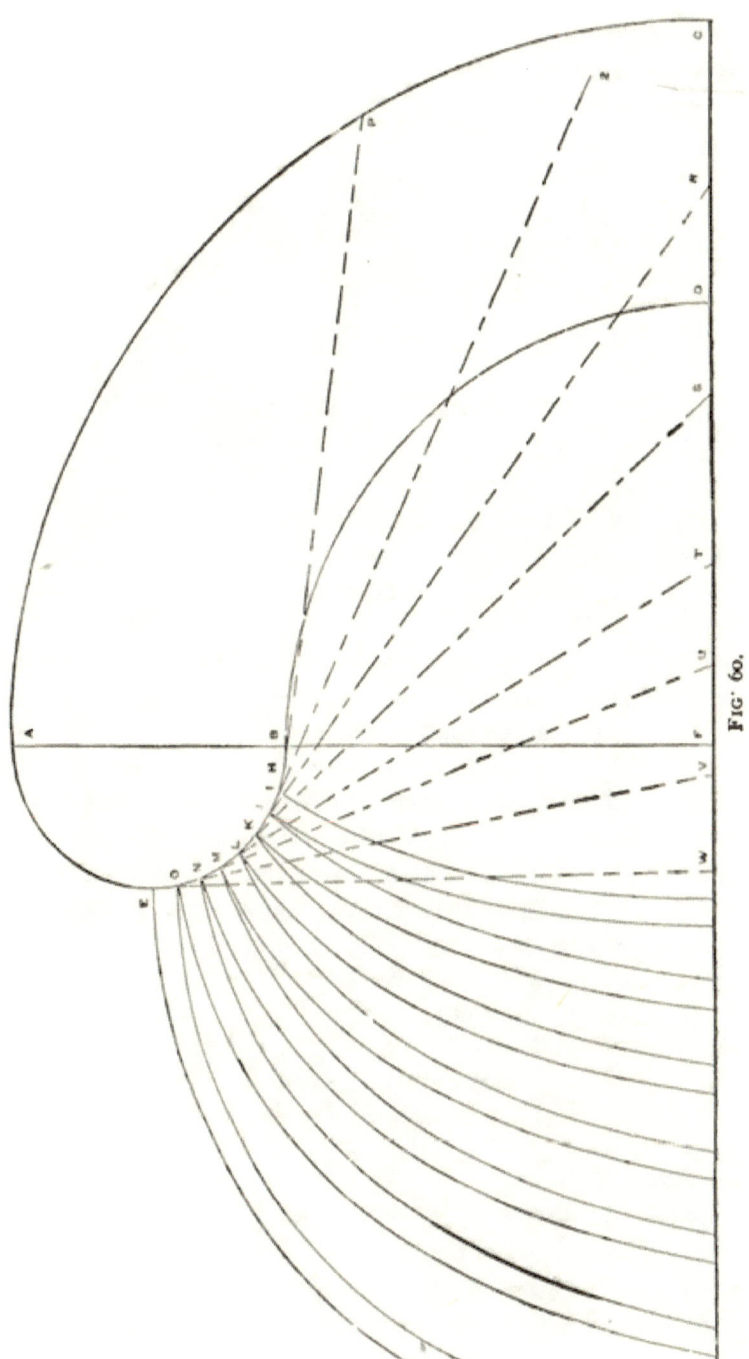

FIG. 60.

wrought to the semicircular curve, A E B, we proceed to
lay out the boards. Divide the quarter circle or quadrant
into nine equal parts, as B H, H I, I J, J K, K L, L M, M N,
N O and O E. Join these points of division by lines, and
produce them till they meet the line G C. Now with R as
centre and J as radius strike the arc shown, also with R as
centre and K as radius strike another arc. With S as centre and S K as radius strike an arc, also with I as centre
strike another. Next take T as centre, and continue in this
way until there is a board for each division in the semicircle. These boards can be cut in short lengths and
joined on the several frames by butt joints, but these butt
joints must be on the radius lines. On account of the difficulty of removing a small centre of this kind, I would suggest that builders, if they desire to use the centre on
another corner, have only a short section made, as A B C D,
Fig. 59. By this means they can build the entire curved
arch in short sections, and move the centre for each as
required; but where it is possible, the best way is to construct the whole centre, and knock it to pieces when the
arch is turned and the mortar set.

In regard to building manholes, which are necessary on
all street sewers, there seems to be one way which almost
all masons follow; that is, to use guide lines stretched from
templates in the manner represented in the drawing,
Fig. 61. Sewers are fitted with chambers placed at convenient distances for the purpose of cleaning and examina-
tion, and they are connected with the street level by a brick
manhole, so that they can be entered by men and worked at.
They are generally built in the shape shown in Fig. 61, or
to a section of truncated cone, this being considered the
strongest form for the purpose, and the brick structure is
topped or covered with a cast-iron cap and removable cover
set flush with the street level. To make the templates or
moulds required is a very simple operation, though it involves the principle before described, and consists in making
two disks or rings of the diameter called for in the engineer's
plans and specifications, one for the bottom and one for the

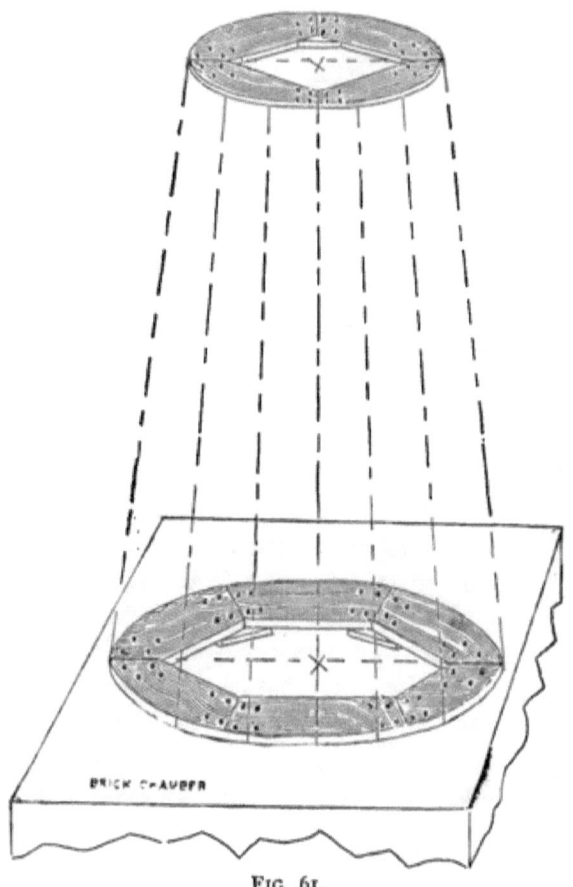

BRICK CHAMBER

FIG. 61.

top.   The top template is supported at the necessary height and set level, and the bottom template is placed on the circular opening in the chamber below, and the lines are fastened to the edges of each template from nails driven into them.   The mason or bricklayer carries up his courses of brick level, turning them round these lines as he goes up.

CHAPTER XI.

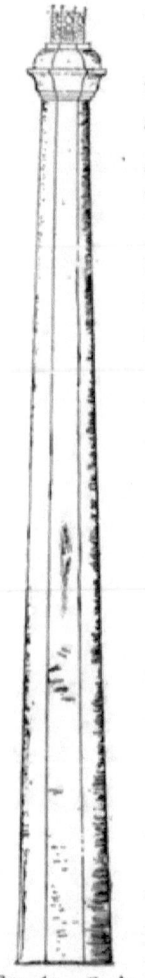

THERE is so little to be said about making plumb rules—in fact, it is such a simple tool for any ordinary carpenter to make, that it seems almost superfluous to touch on the subject, still I think there is one which is more difficult to make than would be supposed, and I think the information will come in handy to many mechanics and builders. The plumb rule which carpenters and masons usually carry and employ is only applicable when the work is to be carried up perfectly perpendicular or plumb. Consequently the two edges are equidistant or parallel, and the gauged line in the centre (over which is stretched the plumb line sustaining the bob or weight) is also parallel to both edges, and when it is applied against the work, either on posts or brick walls, the line must swing exactly to the gauge line before the work can be called exactly plumb. There are, however, structures and details of construction embraced within the art of building which are not built perpendicular from their base or foundation, but for various reasons diminish as they rise. This form is generally adopted where the structure is carried up to a great height, as steeples, spires, towers and factory chimney stacks, for the purpose of lessening the area of resistance to the wind, increasing the area of the base, and di-

FIG. 62.—Scale 1–32.

minishing to the top, where the strain is greater than at
the base. It follows, therefore, that the mechanic must
contrive the diminishing plumb rule. Supposing A to be
the design for an octagonal factory chimney, which is to be

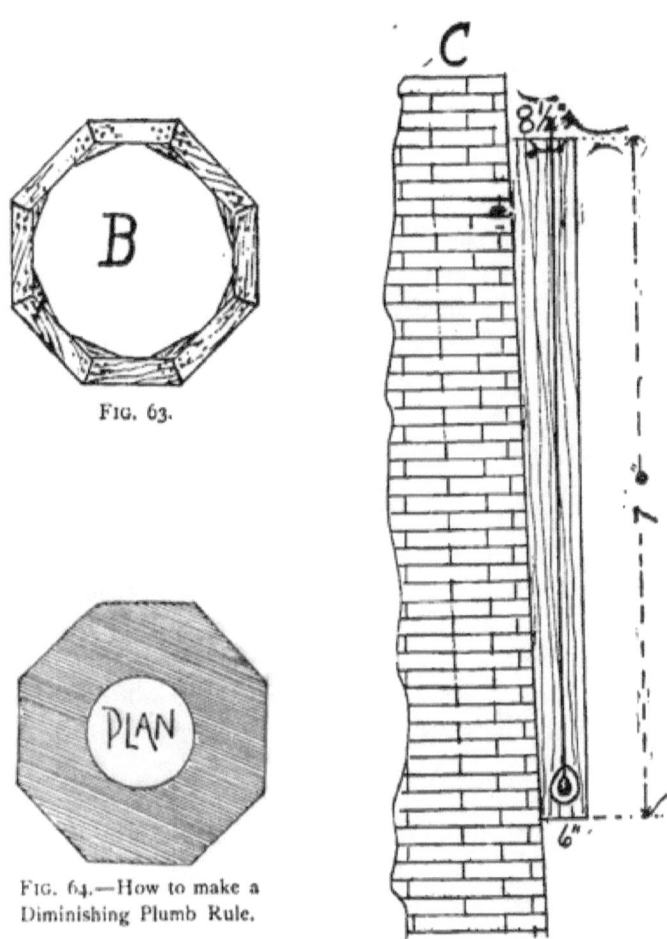

FIG. 63.

FIG. 64.—How to make a
Diminishing Plumb Rule.

FIG. 64.—One-half Inch Scale.

erected in close proximity to a factory, how is it to be
started and carried up to the outline drawn by the architect
and what is the arrangement for doing it?   It is comparatively simple and readily comprehended.   The first thing

to be done is to very carefully take all the measurements, which must not be done to scale, but will be figured out on the details by the architect. This stack is 16 ft. wide at the ground line and diminishes to 8 ft. at the top, below the cornice or top. Now, the carpenter's duty is to construct a wooden template mould or pattern, as B, exactly to the measurement on the plans for the outside form, and a semi or full circular mould for the base or shaft inside, so that the bricklayer may mark this shape on the top side of the foundation and lay his brick neatly to it. This process will give the octagonal form to lay the first course by, and from this the other courses are continued one on top of another until the top is reached. When the template is made the plumb rule is next needed. This is made out of a $1\frac{1}{4}$ in. clear white pine board, faced up out of wind, gauged to $1\frac{1}{16}$ in. thickness, and must be wide enough to make the required rule. One edge shall be jointed perfectly straight by using a straight-edge on it, and shall be squared. The architect's detail will give the angle of diminution, so this angle must be marked off from the bottom squared end of the rule, which may be any convenient width, say four or six inches, or wide enough to permit a hole to be made for the bob to swing, and rise on the board to the length the mason likes best—four, six or seven feet. When this is done the board is gauged parallel to the jointed edge, a hole cut for the bob and saw kerf made to hold the string at the top end. The enlarged sketch C shows a diminishing plumb rule placed against the side or face of the stack, with its left side diminishing and its right plumb. This rule is 7 ft. long, 6 in. wide at the bottom, and $8\frac{1}{4}$ in. at the top, or the diminution is $2\frac{1}{4}$ in. in 7 ft. The entire outline of the whole stack depends upon the plumb rule and the way it is used; therefore, I cannot insist too strongly on its being made extremely accurate and to the angle laid down. It is a very good plan to draw the line to scale the length or height of the intended rule and space the diminish off, or the architect should state the diminish as 1 in. in 5 ft., 2 in. in 7 ft., and so on.

Another thing often requisite in a rule of this kind is to make it slightly hollow on the working edge so as to curve the outline of the chimney and give it a graceful contour. In concluding, I would say that too much care and attention cannot be bestowed on special tools of this nature, as a miscalculation or error may cause very serious consequences.

CHAPTER XII.

IT should be the care of every builder when furring out walls by studding, for the boxing for shutters, to see that they are kept far enough back from the line of the edge of the casing to permit the back linings to go easily into the groove of the casings. Sometimes a great deal of time is lost by the carpenter being obliged to hew off the studs, in order to get the back linings into their place, which ought never to occur. It is much better to have them a little too far back than too far forward, as a strip can always be nailed on the stud to fill up the deficiency.

When no elbows and shutters are used, or when the panel-back comes flush with the plaster and fair with the edges of the jambs, which are also flush with the plaster, the panel-back must be scribed down to the floor, keeping the stiles plumb, so that the rail will sit level, and the top rail fit under the foot-bead, which is rebated out to receive its thickness. Before nailing in position, a straight-edge is placed down the edges of the jambs resting on the floor, and the floor marked. Measure back and mark the thickness of the panel-back, and nail a strip on the floor to prevent the panel-back from driving back whilst nailing. Next place it in its place under the foot-bead, and nail it through the bead into the top edge, and toe-nail the bottom rail into the floor.

When this is done the trim can be put on, but the line of the face of the jambs must be marked down on the face of the panel-back, so that the base blocks and casings can be nailed on the same line.

In front windows which have inside shutters a longer

operation has to be gone through. The first thing done is
to cut out the dados in the window frame, then to take a
rebate plane, shaving off the tongues of the soffit and back
linings together. The soffit is usually ploughed to admit
a tongue on the end of the back lining.

When nailed, the three are driven tightly into the
ploughing on the frame and toe-nailed into the casings,
care being taken to see they are not too wide for the plaster. If this be so, then the soffit must be made narrower by
taking the same stuff off both edges, so that the rails of the
soffit may show of equal width when the tongue on the
inside is driven into the groove in the head casing.
Should the back linings be panelled they must be reduced
in a similar way, so that they will come flush with the plaster. The elbows are then nailed to the panel-back in the
grooves which are prepared for them, placed in the window
recess, and scribed to the floor, so that the edge of top rail
will come exactly to the bottom of the groove in the inside
casing nailed on the sill, in order that the ⅜ in. thick foot-
bead will fit into the groove and close down to the top edge
of the panel-back. After jointing off the top edges of the
panel-back and elbows, the three can now be nailed to the
floor and the foot-bead fitted into the groove on top of the
panel-back, and it returns into the grooves on the back
lining on the top edges of the elbows. After all the above
has been completed the trim can be nailed on as before.
When shutters are used the groove on the inside casing is
generally far enough back from the face of the jamb to
allow space for the combined thickness of the shutter and
back folds and a ½ in. margin outside the shutter, and the
elbows are on the same line as the shutter, so that the foot-
bead breaks the joint.

The best way to scribe the panel-back or panel-backs and
elbows to the floor is as follows:

As it often happens that the frame has been thrown out
of square by the settlement of the building, necessitating
more labor, proceed, after jointing, to place the panel-back
against the frame in the recess, and plumb one stile by

furring up whichever side is low. Set a pair of compasses from the top edge of the casing to the bottom of the groove on whichever corner of the frame is highest, and scribe to the floor. After scribing, it will be found that the corner to which the compasses have been set will come exactly right, but the other side must be planed off until it comes flush with the under side of the groove.

Another suggestion which I would like to offer is this:

To furr out for the skirting before the plaster is put on, as it will save (when it is on) a lot of time digging off the plaster for the furring. Again, to see that the framers get their door and window studs exactly plumb both ways. It will expedite the setting of the door jambs, and save more plaster cutting. Builders will as a rule generally find that a little care in setting up the ground work will save much time when the finish is being put on.

CHAPTER XIII

ONE of the most important and too often neglected things in setting jambs is to block behind the jambs for the screws of the hinges. In rebated jambs this blocking is indispensable; so measure down about 6 in. from the head and 9 in. from the floor, and nail in a 4 in. pine block on the stud, behind the jambs, to secure the screws. Builders should watch sub-contractors in this small matter, as the screws pull out when they have no thickness to hold to.

If the casing have a beaded or moulded edge without corner blocks, the top corners should be mitred with a mitre jack made in the following simple manner:

Take a piece of 1¼ in. stuff, and 1 in. or so wider than the width of the casing, about 2 ft. 6 in. long, nail a fence or piece of ⅞ in. strip on both edges, rising above the surface the thickness of the casing. Now take a bevel, set it exactly—not nearly, but exactly—to an angle of forty-five degrees, or from 3 in. to 5 in. on the steel square (reverse the bevel to see if the angle be true), and mark two reverse mitres across the edges of the ⅞ in. strips and the surface of the bottom or wide piece and over one edge—the edge which has the short corners of the bevels. Saw deep enough into the wide piece on this marked edge to cut through the bead or moulding on the casing when it is placed between the fences against the one which is sawn into. After putting the casing in its place, and marking the top corner with a knife, the casing is placed against the fence with the mark exactly at the saw cut, and having the saw outside the mark so as to slightly leave it on the stuff. The mitre can be readily and instantly sawn without using

5

a bevel or a template, which is inaccurate and unmechani-
cal. The bottom end must fit tightly down on the upper
end of the case block; if not, then the end must be scribed
to the block with the compasses before mitring.

All casings ought to be level across the face, so that
when a straight-edge is placed across the opening it will
touch all their surfaces. The head should also be
straight with the stiles, and all the mitres and joints
tightened and well nailed. All mouldings and back bands
can be mitred and nailed on when the above is done, and
the mitres will come tight.

In setting back window jambs, or on those window
frames which have outside blinds with a panel-back below
the sill, the following is the best way to proceed.

First, cut with a chisel on a straight line the groove
(where it stops against the sides) out of the frame casing,
both top and bottom, on both right and left casing, and
clean all the mortar and dirt out of the ploughing. Now
take the short rebated jamb for the head, and, getting upon
a high horse, place it with its rebated tongue on the head
groove, and mark exactly, with a sharp knife, the inside
corner on the left and right-hand groove. Square these
marks over the face and lay out a dado $\frac{3}{8}$ in. wide toward
each end. Dado this laying out $\frac{3}{8}$ in. deep. Next take
the right and left jamb and square one end of each in pairs.
Lay out a tongue $\frac{3}{8}$ in. wide from these square ends and
$\frac{3}{8}$ in. thick, gauged from the faces. Cut these tongues out
and run a rebate-plane shaving off the back side of the
tongues of the head jamb and sides, and take an arris of
the face side. This will let the tongue go easily into the
grooves in the frame. Next nail the head on the sides,
keeping the front edges flush, and break off the over length
of tongue on the head piece. Set the tongues of the jambs
in the frame grooves, and drive the jambs in till they
sound solid. Use a block, so as not to bruise the edge
when driving. When they are in solid, mark the groove
at the sill, and see if the jambs are not too wide for the
plaster; if they are, the over-wood must be sawn or planed

off until they come flush with the plaster. Take the jambs down when this is done, and lay out a ⅜ in. dado from the groove mark. This dado is to receive the foot-head. Then take the foot-head, cut it to the length of the dados of the head, and ⅜ in. for a tongue on each end. Work these tongues on ⅜ in. deep, and nip the foot-head to the width of the jambs. Ease the tongue as well as the jambs, and nail the head side and foot-head together afterwards; set them up in their place, and when they are driven home toe-nail them into the casing.

When setting door jambs on underflooring, or where the finishing floor is not yet laid, always take the following precautions:

First, place a straight-edge across the floor to each stud at each opening to ascertain if the weight of partition has not sunk it out of level.

Second, ask the foreman if there are base blocks on the trim.

Now if there are, base blocks and the base must be kept level. Supposing one opening has the floor sunk a ½ in. below the level, and another 1 in. below, the difficulty will be to set the jambs so that each base block will be level with the other, and the door heads their proper height and level. In such a case proceed as follows:

The height of the doors being determined by one 8′ 6″ clear of head and floor and one 9′ 6″, nail the heads and jambs together and tack a piece across the edges of the jambs about 12 in. from the bottom, equally distant from the head, about 7′ 6″ down, and keep the jambs parallel by marking the piece with the pencil equal to the inside distance at the head. This being done, obtain a 10 ft. rod and lay off 8′ 7½″ for the 8′ 6″ jambs, and mark this length on one edge of each jamb. This mark will be the scribe line for the jambs, or their exact length. Set them in the opening between the studs, and place a true level on the strip, and wedge up the lowest side until the bulb is exactly in the centre. Now set your compasses to the line on the stile resting on the floor, and keeping the jambs about plumb, scribe them to the floor; saw these lines, always leaving the line on, and replace the jambs far out from the studs, and nail them perfectly plumb and straight on the face. Be sure they are perfectly straight, and wedge out all short crooks and lumps. There is too much careless jamb-setting just now, and one has only to fit a few doors to find this out. Also keep them square to the edges, and be sure they are not nailed in wind.

The object of nailing on the strip is, that by tacking it on equally distant from the head and levelling it the head is likewise levelled without the trouble of climbing upon a horse. The ¼ in. being added to the length brings the head up ½ in. higher, so that the base will come level with the top of the base block on the trim.

The 9′ 6″ jambs are set in the same way, except that 1 in. is allowed 9′ 8″ instead of ½ in. The extra one inch on the length is 8′ 7″, 9″ 7′ is to allow for the finishing floor 1 in. thick. This method should always be followed for first-class trim when there is a supervising architect who uses his eyes. In trimming doors, the trim now comes to the building put together, or with the stiles and head casing glued and dowelled perfectly square, fitted and varnished or polished, all ready to nail up; so it is absolutely necessary that the jambs be properly set and their edges levelled to insure the joints being close.

Jambs should never be set too wide for the thickness of the wall, as in a great many cases no wall moulding is employed, and the back joints must fit to the plaster. They must also be out of wind. In nailing on trim care should be taken to have the margin on the edge showing equal all round, for it often occurs that the trim may be put together, and $\frac{1}{16}$ in. more or less than the dimensions shown on the details; therefore, if only a ⅛ in. is shown on the stiles, the same must be left on the head. One thing in particular must be well done—namely, to fur well under the back edges of all casings and corner blocks, and to fit the wall mould close, as the recesses left by careless-ness in this respect are too often the abodes of vermin.

CHAPTER XIV

THE following information may prove useful to those carpenters who have never worked hardwood, and who may be suddenly given a job to do. When nailing, never drive cut-iron nails without first boring for them. A German bit is the best to use; they cut clean and easy, and pull out the cores. Wire nails, however, are best for the work, and if the wood be very hard, as heart ash or quartered oak, the point should be dipped in wax or soap. A very convenient grease-box can be made by boring a ⅜ in. hole in the haft of a hammer, and filling it up with wax or soap; it is always at hand, and not in the way. When nailing in panel moulding, never drive the nail so slanting that it will go into the panel, but keep it nearly parallel with the face of the panel, so that the nail will enter the edge of the stile rail or muntin. By driving it thus, it will hold the moulding on the frame; but if it goes into the panel, when the panel shrinks the moulding will draw away from the edge, and likely split the panel.

When possible, nail all work so that the nail-holes will cover. For instance, when setting jambs nail through the edges into the studding, as polished or varnished work showing the natural wood is marred by nailing through the face. If it must be nailed on the face as trimming, be very careful not to split the work, and use a small pointed set. Be sure there is no grease left on the face of the hammer after each nail is driven, because it is liable to bend the next nail. The best way to make inside joints with hardwood is to scribe them. Often the stuff is warped, and cutting a square joint only means fitting,

which can be avoided by scribing the joint. If it is com-
pulsory to nail back a piece of very much twisted stuff, like
hazel or sycamore, the mechanic should be very cautious,
for kiln-dried timber is so brittle and non-elastic that it will
not readily yield to strain and will crack like glass. The
best plane to use on all hardwood is of course the iron
plane, especially where the wood is curly or cross-grained.
Keep the plane sharp and keen. Dull tools may do fairly
well on pine, but on hardwood they are useless; so keen
edges are indispensable for clean work, so that little scraping need be done. A good iron block plane is also necessary, but I would recommend all cuts and mitres to be
made direct from the saw. A good workman will make
his calculations carefully, and insure the certainty of his
cut before making it.

Finally, proceed carefully and steadily, and don't bang
the work with the hammer. Use a block if you must drive
the stuff, so as not to mark it, and make a good, clean job.

CLAMPING.

How many men are there in our carpenter shops nowa-
days who can systematically and perfectly glue and clamp
up a stub-tenon door? There are very few indeed, and a
great many faulty joints can be attributed to the very want
of this necessary knowledge. Clamping, especially in the
case of hardwood or veneered doors, shutters, etc., should
be done rapidly and perfectly, in order that the glue may
be enabled by the auxiliary means employed to assist its
operation to properly perform its function. The usual
method employed is to take the framed door apart, place
the stiles together face to face, and put them, mortised
edge down, in the hot box. Similarly, all the rails and
mortises are heated to the same temperature as the hot box.
When heated, the stiles are first taken out, the mortised
edges turned up, and the mortises are smeared inside with
glue (moderately thick), also the relishes and shoulders.
The mortises for muntins in the rails, or in the muntins,
if there be any, are also smeared, then the tenons and tusks.

Put in the bottom rail first, face side to face side of stile, keeping the face edge to laying-out mark on stile; then slip in your panel, if it goes in without any fillet, and insert the muntin in bottom rail mortise. Drive in all the rails and muntins in this manner, and when all are in, turn the whole upside down, and, inserting the other tenons in the second stile, slam the door down on the bench to bring the shoulders to their place. Drop the door on the clamps, and quickly give all the clamps a turn to squeeze out the glue. Slack them back again, and adjust a tail clamp lengthways over the muntins. Place the muntins exactly to the laying-out mark, and squeeze them to tighten joints on the rails. Keep the rails perfectly square to the stiles, or the joints will never hold, and screw the clamps hard, carefully watching that the joints do not spring up or start the veneer, also that the door does not wind or raise up from the clamps. Expedition and a little care will insure a good job, and the latent heat in the wood will keep the glue from setting until the parts are together.

CHAPTER XV.

BUILDERS throughout the country in their daily practice find it necessary to erect temporary scaffolding,
and in doing so usually employ scrap stuff, or some of the
material they intend using in the building. These scaffolds
require to be handy, take little time in constructing, and
must at the same time be strong and suitable for safely sustaining men and material. With a view to assist builders
to a rapidly formed system of scaffolding the following is
submitted:

The handiest, though not always the most applicable
form, is the bracket scaffold, which consists of a number of
permanently framed timber brackets, placed on a line, at a
convenient distance apart, on which to rest the planks.
Each bracket measures about 4 × 4 ft., and is framed together
of 1½ in. or 2 × 3 in. sound spruce, for lightness and
strength. It is held in its place on the frame wall by a
¾ in. round iron bolt, which is forged long enough to pass
through the boarding and studding, and a 2 in. block,
which spans two studs inside. The end of the bolt is tapped,
and the bracket can be screwed tight against the boarding by a screw, key and washer. The bolt is fastened to
the bracket under the horizontal arm, after passing through
a hole in the vertical arm, by being forged flat and bored
and bolted to it with ¼ in. bolts, which are countersunk on
the upper side of the arm, to permit the plank to rest level
on it.

All that is required to affix these brackets to the building
is to bore a hole for the bolt, and they hang quite safe, and
will sustain the weight of any ordinary quantity of boards

or siding. They can also be put up for boarding, and taken down as each strip of covering is finished.

In the absence of the above, a good safe scaffold can be quickly made of joists and $\frac{7}{8}$ in. covering or roofing boards. Cleats gained out the thickness of the bracket board are first got out, and to the gain a bracket piece is well nailed; the outer end of the bracket piece is next nailed square to the side of a sound joist at the required height, and the three together are then nailed by the cleat through the wall boarding into a stud. If much weight is to be put on the scaffold, blocks should be nailed under the bracket piece on the vertical joist to take the strain off the nails, especially when hemlock joists are used for uprights.

A very simple way of gaining a strong scaffold is to lay joists on their edges across brackets no more than ten feet apart, with ledgers placed across their upper edges, on which the planks rest. It is also very convenient when the scaffolding planks are not forthcoming, and boards are substituted, and it saves a double thickness of boards. This scaffold is braced diagonally, and, in order to increase its height, another joist can be placed on the top end of the bottom one, and the joist secured by nailing a $\frac{7}{8}$ cleat across it.

A useful and easily removed scaffold for putting on roof boarding consists of simple brackets nailed through the roof boarding into the rafters beneath, with a plank laid across them to stand on.

When the boarding is all on, and the window frames and cornice set, one of the next accessories is a handy shingling stage. After the first courses have been laid, it is usual to form a scaffold out of joist laid against the roof on their edge, and fastened by shingles. The best way, however, is to shingle the joist in, by nailing the shingles to it, and fastening them in a course of shingles, keeping those nailed on the joist down, so that the joist will come below the butts of those in the course. These can be cut off when the scaffold is no longer needed, and the roof will not have been in any way injured.

The handiest scaffold which a carpenter and builder can

adopt for setting cornices over store fronts, consists of a piece of 8 or 9 by 1 in. spruce board nailed square across near the ends of two joists at the desired height, far enough apart to permit each joist to stand respectively, allowing for the difference in their levels on the store floor and side-walk. When the number of these frames needed is nailed together, they are placed in position, braced diagonally, and the plank laid across them. This method makes a very convenient, firm scaffold, and costs very little time.

CHAPTER XVI.

FOREMAN carpenters should have a boy or two on the works. They are very handy for running errands, picking up stuff, etc.

If possible, keep all your scaffolding plant in stock and in good order. Do not waste time on improvised scaffolds, unless they can't possibly be avoided.

Builders should be careful to see that their masons, when building chimneys in frame structures, do not sustain any part of the brickwork on the timber construction, because all brickwork settles to a more or less extent, and should the whole weight of a chimney-stack be brought to bear on lower floor beams, it will surely bear it down and throw it out of level.

When lumber is placed adjacent to the side of a prospective building, always see that it is stacked so that the air will circulate round each piece and season it thoroughly. Framing pieces should be regularly built up in level piles, with strips between each stick or layer of sticks. Boards, as flooring, sheathing, siding or clapboarding, should be stacked in triangular stacks or kept in extemporized sheds. They should never be allowed to twist or warp, or be exposed to the sun's rays or rain.

When laying rough floor, or under floor, in good work, if double floors are used, always lay it diagonally, as it will be found more economical for the following reasons: First, when the finished floor is laid it lies evener; second, it is easier laying the finished floor because the under floor does not prevent it from driving together through the unevenness of the joints; third, it binds the building stronger together; and fourth, the time seemingly lost is more than made up in the rapidity in which the finished floor can be laid on top of it.

When raising the frames of buildings, especially those of the balloon type, it is absolutely necessary to brace them thoroughly in order that the pieces which are already in position may not·be jarred or strained out of place while raising the other pieces which rest on them. To illustrate this, I might say that when the side walls are up they must be well stayed by board braces, nailed on diagonally at each end, to the sills and posts. It is likewise a judicious practice to rough-board or cover the outside walls before raising the roof, and, when possible, this boarding will be much better if nailed on diagonally. Some maintain that the horizontal boarding is sufficient, and makes a house strong enough to resist any ordinary wind pressure; but the first method not alone makes a stiffer construction, but gives a smoother surface for laying on the clapboarding or siding.

When finished stuff comes to a building ready to be put up, there is often much carelessness displayed in placing it so as to preserve its form and finish. It would be admirable if builders and foremen would consider its cost and future more and place it safely in its proper position. For this reason we put forward the following, which our friends who are builders will, no doubt, recognize as judicious: No inside finish should be brought to a job until it is fully plastered and ready to have it put up. When the base comes, as it is kiln-dried, it should be stacked up with thin strips between each board to allow the air to circulate and keep it as dry as possible in the damp building. All the joined trim and doors should be brought to a job as soon as possible, in order that it may become seasoned as the building dries out, especially the doors, because they are more liable to absorb the dampness inherent in every newly plastered building. In fact, they will absorb a certain amount and swell to a large extent. They should not be fitted while in this condition, but left until the walls are dried out;

so that when they do shrink after fitting, the shrinkage
will be reduced to a minimum. Framed work of all kinds
should therefore be stacked vertically against a wall, to
obviate the danger of twisting, or laid flat, one on top of
another, with strips between each piece and weighted.
A good plan is to shore them down solid from the ceiling
or opposite wall. Another preventive often used is to
first give the stuff a coat of oil filler, or priming coat of
paint, which has the good quality of filling up the open
pores of the kiln-dried material and to a large extent pre-
venting the absorption mentioned above. Veneered work
should also be carefully guarded, and precautions taken to
counteract the effect of the prevalent moisture so destruc-
tive to finely finished work. Varnished work should be
filled and polished work oiled.

I note that many builders are partial to setting their door
and window jambs before the plaster is put on, thus making
their edges grounds, as it were, to straighten the plaster
surfaces. This practice is, to my mind, a mistake, and
some of its consequences show this. Plaster should always
be put on to grounds nailed on the studding, and not to the
edges of finished work.

If you are not already able to draw or lay out a piece of
work full working size from an architect's drawing, I
would recommend you to learn how to do it right away.
No man can do a job as it ought to be done unless he under-
stands the idea the architect intends to convey by his scale
drawing. Another pointer is this: Don't jump to the con-
clusion that the architect's detail is wrong because you
can't work from it. I have found that there are many
men who, as long as things are clear to them, are all
right, but the moment anything arises which seems com-
plicated or difficult, they will not stop to solve it, but
rush off to the architect, complaining that such and such
a thing wont work out. If you can't understand it at first,
lay it aside for a while, and when you have leisure, as at
noon hour, quietly think it out. Then if it wont work
itself out, see the architect and have it fully explained.

Be sure, when putting on siding, that the courses are straight right through, especially when they are long, or over 15 ft. from casing to casing, or corner board to casing, or corner board to corner board. Let me suggest to all who are conscientious that they nail into the studs and not through the sheathing, as water will surely go through and rot both siding and boards.

I see a good many men using a level to plumb their posts and studding with. This looks all right, but it isn't the proper way. The proper way is to use a good plumb rule, as long as can be handled, with a heavy lead bob on it. By this means, if the post be lumpy on the surface or not quite straight, the long straight-edge of the rule will more likely keep it correct than a short level two or two and one-half feet long. This applies also to levelling sills. Don't place the level right on the sill, but use a long, parallel straight-edge, and block up the sill until it touches the edge right through.

I know of no quality so essential to make a successful mechanic as self-confidence, and this as a rule only comes from ability. I would therefore recommend all carpenters to become as expert as possible.

Allow me to warn carpenters against the indiscriminate use of the claw on the hammer. When you have to pull a bent or broken nail out in nailing up trim or finish of any kind, don't take a leverage with the head directly on the smooth surface of the stuff, but place a block under the head. It gives more leverage, prevents the surface being bruised, and likewise shows a careful workman.

Mortise locks ought never to be set into the door stile too tight, because when they don't fit easy the plates are pressed inward and the movable parts inside are jammed and turn hard. A ⅝ in. mortise lock ought therefore to be bored for with a ¾ in. auger bit, ¾ in. with a ⅞ in., and so on. The mortise should be cut straight with the surfaces parallel to the faces of the door stile, in order that the edges of the face plate may likewise be parallel to the arrises formed by the junction of the faces and edge.

Let me give builders a pointer about floors which they should remember. Don't lay your finish floors till all the mechanics are out of the house, and when they are laid cover them carefully with paper. Another one is: Always keep your stairs covered with paper and boards until the job is finished, as it is a pity to see hardwood treads all scratched up, which will, of course, show through the finish.

When you are fitting doors don't make the top joint too close, for in a new job the walls will settle down, and they can't be opened. Always cut the stiles on pine doors about $\frac{1}{16}$ in. short, so that when the top rail shrinks it will come back flush with the ends of the stiles. If you have to bend, base, or chair-rail around corners, kerf it from the back, and do it systematically by spacing the kerfs equally, in order that the piece will bend without breaking. I used to wet my stuff, which made it more flexible and yielding, and when nailing it on I either shored or bracketed it in from opposite wall or floor.

As I see the use of the saddle or threshold on inside doors is going out of date, in order to allow the carpet to pass from one room to another without having to cut it, I would recommend that when you are fitting doors that you leave the bottom edge of the outside corner an eighth of an inch shorter than the hanging side corner.

There are many men who express different opinions about iron and wood planes. Now, as far as my experience goes, and it extends over many years' continuous work, I think the iron plane is good on ash, oak, maple, sycamore, cherry, butternut, satinwood, rosewood, mahogany, walnut, etc., as, being always close in the mouth and capable of being finely set on the edge, it lessens the danger of tearing out the grain, which is so great in open-mouthed wooden planes; but they must be nicely set and handled, or they leave a mark which will incur much labor to take out with scraper. Here I would say a word about scrapers, as opinions about sharpening these tools differ somewhat. Some say the only way to sharpen a scraper is to file the edge perfectly straight and square to the sides, and then turn up the arris with a smooth file or round side of a gauge. This is a very good way, but a better one, I think, is to grind the edge with a basil like a plane iron and whet it upon an oil-stone till it lifts a shaving like a plane iron or bit. I used to use a wood stock on my scraper, to save my hand from getting blistered or raw when I had much scraping to do.

A very good method to bend such trimming stuff as chair rail, base, necking, etc., is to place the piece in water over night. This makes it soft and easily bent, so it can be turned into simple or compound curves of any radius. This also helps when kerfing stuff round curves, as it tends to make the wood more elastic.

Sycamore and hazel base will need to have wood plugs driven in the joints of the brick, and vertical strips, the thickness of the plaster, nailed on, to hold it securely in position.

I cannot recommend the method of fastening mantels to chimney breasts by nailing a strip to the brickwork under the shelf. A better method would be to plug and then nail the strip to the plugs, but care must be taken to drive no wood into the flues.

www.ingramcontent.com/pod-product-compliance
Lightning Source LLC
Chambersburg PA
CBHW030002030726
47499CB00008B/2859